ENVIRONMENT AND AMERICANS

ENVIRONMENT AND AMERICANS

The Problem of Priorities

Edited by **RODERICK NASH**
University of California, Santa Barbara

HOLT, RINEHART AND WINSTON
New York • Chicago • San Francisco • Atlanta
Dallas • Montreal • Toronto • London • Sydney

Cover illustrations: Top, Swan Lake in Western Montana *(Montana Highway Commission)*; bottom, aerial view of New York City *(Port of New York Authority)*

CONTENTS

Aerial view of Los Angeles suburb. (Geotronics).

INTRODUCTION

In 1836 Ralph Waldo Emerson published a little essay entitled "Nature" that delineated the conflicting priorities that have shaped American attitudes toward the environment. The attitudes, in turn, shaped the American environment itself. On the one hand, Emerson observed, nature could be "commodity." In this utilitarian role it served man's needs for clothing, building materials, and food. But for Emerson the environment had many other—he would say "higher" —uses. Among these were "beauty," "language," "discipline" and, at the opposite end of the spectrum of priorities from "commodity," moral laws and spiritual truth. "Nature," Emerson triumphantly concluded, "is the symbol of spirit."

Of course not everyone agreed with the Transcendentalists, particularly in 1836. "For one that comes with a pencil to sketch or sing," Henry David Thoreau remarked a few years later after a trip to the Maine woods, "a thousand come with an axe or rifle."

The competing claims to the American environment that Emerson and Thoreau described did not come into sharp conflict until the twentieth century. Previously the sheer size of the New World and its abundance of resources settled most controversies before they began. There was enough for everyone. The environment easily met a variety of demands. But the era of easy pickings and unlimited space screeched to a halt in the 1890s as American expansion bounced off the west coast to fill the last habitable "islands" of land. The decade began with the United States Census matter-of-factly informing the nation that it no longer had a frontier. In 1893 historian Frederick Jackson Turner underscored the significance of this fact in a paper that linked the frontier experience and American characteristics and institutions.

For Turner and his contemporaries a frontierless America raised many troublesome questions. The violent strikes and riots of the 1890s and the depression that seized the economy confirmed people's fears. It seemed that the future would be increasingly one of man pitted against man rather than against nature. In terms of the environment this meant increased competition among priorities. A tree, for example, could not serve the lumberman and the poet simultaneously. A valley could not be both the site of an open pit mine and an object of aesthetic and spiritual veneration. Or could it? If one's loyalties were to lumber and mines—and the civilization they supported—then the development of wil-

1

derness *was* venerable. For the disciples of wildness, to be sure, the same development was desecration.

The "problem" of concern in this book is less of an issue among American historians and more one among Americans themselves that historians have recorded. It is a debate in the American mind that extends to the very roots of our civilization. Ultimately the environmental problem demands a judgment about that civilization itself. The American environment of the early seventeenth century was, essentially, a clean slate. Men wrote upon it (built a civilization) according to their values, their religion, their aesthetic standards, their definition of progress, and their vision of the good life. The study of environmental history consequently reveals important truths about American thought and action. The landscape, rightly seen, is just as important an historical document as the printed page. While the one is marked with ink, the other bears the impress of axe and bulldozer. We know how to decipher the former; we are just beginning to "read" the environment.

It would be comparatively easy to discuss Americans and environment if opinions were pure and neatly confined to individuals or factions. But this chess-game approach distorts the way we actually think about the environment. Ambivalence characterizes our viewpoint. Wilderness, for example, is desirable but so is civilization. We want both lumber and trees. The choice is almost always between two goods, not between good and bad. And the contest is usually fought within rather than between individual minds. For instance, most wilderness enthusiasts do not wish to return to cave living nor would the proponents of civilization really wish to pave parks and paint them green. Environmental attitudes, in sum, must be seen as kaleidoscopic patterns of changing priorities. Often frustrating to study, the subject is for the same reason a rich source of information about the nuances of American thought.

In studying the following selections look for the nature and sources of the environmental biases of the people discussed. Also be aware of your own opinions. Reading this book should be an exercise in self-understanding as well as in the understanding of American history.

You will begin to approach the problem of concern by investigating the environmental attitudes of part of the first wave of American settlers. Peter N. Carroll's discussion of the Puritan pioneers shows how ideas and actions exerted a mutual influence on the mind of the seventeenth century. It is not easy from our present vantage point, but try to understand what it meant to occupy a tiny speck of civilization on the edge of a vacant continent. Of course Indians were present, but for the Puritans and most pioneers they were a form of wild animal who increased, rather than lessened, the wildness of the environment. Also make an effort to sympathize with the Puritans' fear of reverting to barbarism. On the edge of the wilderness it was essential to keep strict standards lest controls be sloughed off entirely. A revealing question to bring to the Carroll essay is "how do you think the Puritans would have reacted to a proposal for a national park and wilderness preserve?" Keep Carroll's essay in mind as you read the next two. Contact with wilderness produced a common set of environmental attitudes in people far apart geographically and intellectually. Whether in Massachusetts in 1620, Pennsylvania in 1720, Illinois in 1820, or Alaska in 1920, the pioneer perspective was essentially the same. Try to discover its major components from the readings.

Alan Trachtenberg goes beyond the Puritan experience to frame some generalizations about the American and the environment. Note carefully the characteristics and history of the two principal positions Trachtenberg delineates. Did pastoralism represent a real option for Americans? To what extent was it a means of assuaging the guilt incurred in destroying pastoral conditions?

The initial group of readings ends with a selection from Stewart Udall, a former Secretary of the Interior, concerning the history of the golden age of resource exploitation. You should notice the priorities that underlay the greatest barbeque of the American environment. These values are important because in the last analysis men, not machines, rape the land. Not saws, in other words, but the men who wield them and the society that makes their efforts profitable are the causative agents. This is the meaning of Pogo's comment that in regard to environmental deterioration "we have met the enemy and he is us." The remark is a reminder that the viewpoint Udall describes did not vanish with the frontier. Pioneers in white collars and business suits still ride what remains of the range while their spiritual brothers ride spaceships to the stars.

Even a cursory glance at the history of "conservation" in the United States is enough to ascertain that the word has little or no meaning. Like "peace" and "freedom" its banner has been carried by groups (or viewpoints) that are poles apart. The second set of readings is designed to show the varieties of conservation experience. Hans Huth opens the section with an examination of the rise in the nineteenth century of the nonutilitarian or aesthetic interpretation of conservation. This position supported the creation of the first state and national parks. To understand its significance, ask yourself what the people described in the preceding three selections would have thought of the idea of preserving nature for its aesthetic values. Pay special attention to the kind of people Huth discusses. What, in general, are their positions in society, their incomes, their chief places of residence, and what significance do these facts have?

The waning of the nineteenth century brought with it the rise of the urban-industrial civilization we know today. One consequence was a dramatic growth in American society of the attitude toward nature that Huth described. What, according to Peter Schmitt, is the back-to-nature urge? Among what kinds of people did it flourish and for what reasons? Would you say the call of the wild has increased or decreased since the early twentieth century? Use yourself as a document. To what extent do you feel an urge to escape the civilized environment, to "get away from it all"?

Clearly the Americans Schmitt analyzes constituted a reservoir of support

for certain parts of the conservation crusade. But nature enthusiasts and preservationists would not have supported much of the conservation ideology Arthur
Ekirch describes. What priorities do the utilitarian conservationists advance and
how do they differ from those of the back-to-nature faction? Also ask yourself
how the utilitarian conservationists' perspective compares to that of the pioneers.

Grant McConnell's contribution begins by digging deeper into the Progressive conservation movement of the early twentieth century. His purpose is to
assess the reasons for both its successes and failures. Do you agree with Mc-
Connell's analysis? How does McConnell explain the recent surge of concern for
environmental problems? Think of other reasons in your own lifetime for the
growth of concern over environmental irresponsibility. Could it be argued that
the "strong popular base" of the movement to which McConnell refers is explained by a more general reordering of American priorities particularly on the
part of younger members of American society? The statements in the last section
of this book will shed further light on this subject.

In the next two selections David Lowenthal and Richard G. Lillard explore
two varieties of contemporary conservation. Lowenthal is concerned with the
American taste in landscape. Why, he wants to know, do we prefer some scenes
or environments and dislike others? In reading his essay try to discover what is
the essence of his dispute with the wilderness lovers. Pay special attention to
Lowenthal's final sentence. How does it apply to your own environmental
biases? Richard Lillard takes up the delicate problem occasioned by the possibility of loving nature to death. That is to say, those who appreciate a particular
environment can ruin it just as surely as those oblivious or hostile to its charms.
National parks are a case in point. They can be spoiled by success. Lillard describes several varieties of management policy that have been applied to the
parks in the last six decades. Be sure you understand the "circus" approach,
at one extreme, and the preservationist ideal at the other as well as the numerous
compromise policies that are usually employed. Why do you think John Muir
and his associates in the Sierra Club did not realize the danger automobiles posed
to Yosemite Valley? What, in your opinion, are the possibilities for solving the
problems of overuse described in Lillard's essay? In this connection you might
think how you would justify a policy of restricting the public's access to a public
park.

As the previous six selections suggest, the fight *among* conservationists can
be just as bitter as those *between* conservationists and exploiters. Indeed, the principal dynamic of American environmental history in the twentieth century has
come, so to speak, from civil rather than foreign wars. Everyone claims to favor
conservation. But under the pressure of decision-making the consensus rapidly
breaks down, and men who believed themselves to be colleagues find that they
are enemies. In the final selection of this section, Roderick Nash examines the
unhappy history of the relationship between John Muir and William Kent. Their
experience, which may stand for that of many of their countrymen, dramatizes

the lack of agreement on priorities that still plagues conservation. In reading the essay try to determine exactly what is at issue between Muir and Kent. On what are they in agreement? Where do they split apart? What do you think are the possibilities of compromising their differences? In responding to this last question, imagine you are an environmental manager (perhaps the President of the United States) faced with deciding a case like the one involving the Hetch Hetchy Valley that destroyed the friendship of Muir and Kent.

The final group of selections represents an entirely new perspective on environmental problems. Man's needs, even his non-material needs, are subordinated by the ecologists to the well-being of the environment itself. "Ecology" derives from the Greek root "oikos" or house. The essential concept in ecology is the interrelation of all the inhabitants of the house called earth. An ecologist studies these complex dependencies, and puts the long-term survival of the entire life system in the forefront of his environmental priorities.

In recent years the ecological perspective has risen to the forefront of the environment movement in the United States. In the public mind the beginnings of awareness can be traced to 1960, the year Rachel Carson began publication of a series of essays on the adverse effects of insecticides on the balance of nature. Two years later *Silent Spring* became a best-selling book, and the nation discovered ecology. But there is considerable evidence that the first Americans, the Indians, possessed the substance if not the name of ecology. Frank Speck's article makes a case for this assumption. As you read his essay think carefully about the reasons why a so-called primitive culture might have a keener appreciation of its dependency on the environment than a highly civilized one. What other factors (principally religious and economic) make up the difference between Speck's Indian and, for example, Udall's resource exploiters?

While Western civilization has adhered for most of the last two thousand years to a man-*versus*-nature philosophy, Clarence Glacken argues in the next selection that this perspective is not typical of human thought as a whole. The American Indians, not the American pioneer, were in the mainstream of intellectual history. The problem, for Americans, is to recognize this point. How does Glacken's essay help? What do you feel are the chances of an alternative relationship to the environment taking root in American thought as a whole? In considering this question take into account the intellectual, psychological, economic, and political obstacles in the way of full acceptance of the environmental perspective.

For the most part historians have not been as yet closely involved in the national discussion of environment and ecology. In the next essay Wilbur R. Jacobs asks "why not?" According to Jacobs the keepers of the past can play an important role in fostering an ecological perspective by pointing to environmental irresponsibility in the past. How does Jacobs' analysis revise traditional ideas about frontier history? How does it support the belief that every age must rewrite its own history?

Leo Marx also takes a look into the American past to find both the reasons for and a possible solution to the environmental crisis. Take time to read this difficult but important essay carefully, outlining its central theses. Where does Marx lay the blame for environmental irresponsibility? Do you agree? Do you think the scientists to which Marx, a professor of English, addresses his essay would agree?

Another application of history to the environmental crisis is demonstrated in Raymond Dasmann's contribution. By examining the environmental history of California, Dasmann derives the motivation to launch a polemic against thoughtless exploitation and a prescription for stewardship. What kind of environment does Dasmann advocate as optimum for man? What do you think are the methods Americans could use to achieve Dasmann's ideals and the chances of those methods being successful? Notice especially how Dasmann questions many precepts sacred to the chamber-of-commerce mentality. How do you think this mentality would respond to Dasmann's priorities? Pressing this line of inquiry to the extreme, do you think the environment issue holds any potential for starting a civil war in American society? It is instructive in this regard to recall that an important reason for the Civil War of the 1860s was the enslavement of human beings; some now believe the environment is similarly enslaved by the institution of private property and that this too is wrong.

The most thoroughgoing challenge to the pioneer perspective and, in some ways, to the utilitarian rationale of certain conservationists, is contained in the philosophy of Aldo Leopold. A pioneer ecologist and wildlife manager as well as an advocate of wilderness preservation, Leopold began in the 1930s to call for a radically new attitude toward the environment. Susan Flader's discussion of Leopold's thought offers an opportunity to see the way his knowledge of ecology underlies his "land ethic." The essay should also make clear how Leopold, unlike most others in the environment movement, does not in the last analysis put man's welfare first. Be sure you understand what *does* have the top priority in Leopold's system. What consequences for human conduct stem from this point of view?

There is reason for encouragement in a comparison of the priorities set forth by the exponents of an ecological perspective and those employed by the pioneers. The old, potentially suicidal, criteria appear to have weakened. Of course they are far from dead as a look at the morning newspaper or at the environment itself will confirm. The historian is in the best position to testify to the recent and radical nature of the ecological view. He should also be among the most interested in tracing the continuing struggle for existence between the old priorities and man himself.

In the reprinted selections footnotes appearing in the original sources have in general been omitted unless they contribute to the argument or a better understanding of the selection.

Buried in the often turgid rhetoric of the New England Puritans is a rich source of information about early attitudes toward the American environment. PETER N. CARROLL (b. 1943) has probed Puritan thought in an attempt to understand this important aspect of seventeenth-century social and intellectual history. For the most part the people about whom Carroll writes arrived in the New World between 1620 and 1630. Their priorities constitute a yardstick against which later thinking can be measured.

Peter N. Carroll

Puritans and the Transformation of the Wilderness

The transit of European civilization to the New World in the seventeenth century inevitably affected both the transplanted culture and the wilderness environment of America. While the forest influenced New England thought in covert ways, the Puritans radically altered the appearance of the untamed continent which confronted them. . . .

Supporters of the Winthrop expedition of 1630 had emphasized the value of subduing the earth in justification of the migration to New England. Francis Higginson, to promote the settlement of Massachusetts, lamented the sparsity of good Christians "to make use of this fruitful land." It is sad, he informed his friends in England, "to see so much good ground . . . lie altogether unoccupied." "Colonies," asserted John White, "have their warrant from God's direction and command . . . to replenish the earth, and to subdue it." New Englanders rationalized their claims to the Indian lands with similar rhetoric. "The Indians are not able to make use of the one fourth part of the land," observed Higginson, "neither have they any settled places, . . . but change their habitation from place to place." John Cotton assured the departing Winthrop group that whoever "taketh possession of [vacant soil], and bestoweth culture and husbandry upon it" has an inviolable right to the land. In subsequent years, the colonists issued similar appeals to justify the acquisition of wilderness territories. . . .

John Winthrop . . . argued that the

From Peter N. Carroll, *Puritanism and the Wilderness: The Intellectual Significance of the New England Frontier, 1629–1700* (New York: Columbia University Press, 1969), pp. 181–186, 189–195. Footnotes omitted.

Indians possessed "only a natural right to so much land as they had or could improve," and "the rest of the country lay open to any that could and would improve it."

The Puritan colonists resolved from the beginning to transform the wilderness into settled estates. . . . The leaders of New England therefore attempted to base their policy of land distribution upon the ability of people to subdue the earth. In 1634 the General Court of Massachusetts Bay ordered "that if any man hath any great quan[tity] of land . . . and doeth not builde upon it or imp[rove it] within three yeares," the Court may "disp[ense] of it to whome they please." Although New Englanders, like all seventeenth-century Europeans, believed that certain men of quality deserved greater wealth than the masses of society, they nevertheless stressed the necessity of improving the soil before parceling out the land. . . .

Because of the commitment among Puritans to improve waste lands, New Englanders frequently appealed to the value of physically transforming the wilderness in support of inland expansion. The Massachusetts General Court approved the extension of the town of Linn in 1639, provided that the settlers "make some good proceeding in planting" within two years, "so as it may bee a village fit to conteine a convenient number of inhabitants." In 1643 six residents of the town of Concord requested the General Court to grant them "some reasonable quantitie of land" because the area about Concord was "very barren, and the meadows very wet and unuseful." They supported their petition by reminding the authorities that "it is your desire [that] the lands might be subdued" and persuaded the General Court to offer them a plantation "provided that within two

years they make some good improvement of it.". . .

As the government of Massachusetts became reconciled to increased inland extension, would-be frontiersmen justified their desire to remove by reiterating the need to subjugate the wilderness. The founders of Northampton, for example, advised the General Court that their proposed plantation would provide surplus agricultural products for the benefit of the entire colony. Similarly, in 1659 the General Court approved the erection of the town of Hadley in order "that this wildernes may be populated and the maine ends of our coming into these parts may be promoted.". . .

Despite the popular myth of the abundance of natural resources during the seventeenth century, the colonies of New England frequently complained of shortages of wood and enacted legislation to regulate the destruction of trees. The lack of timber was especially acute at the Bay, and in the winter of 1637–38 John Winthrop reported that the inhabitants of Boston "were almost readye to breake up for want of wood." The inland settlements at Springfield, Connecticut, and New Haven also suffered from a paucity of wood and provided laws "for the better preserving of Tymber." The individual town governments controlled the use of common woods and established penalties for violations of these laws. In 1635 the selectmen of Boston regretted the destruction of some nearby wood and provided relief for the poor people who would have benefited from the use of this timber. Such legislation ordinarily reflected the pragmatic concern of a wilderness people for preventing the needless destruction of a valuable commodity. In at least one exceptional case, however, New Englanders employed conservationist rhetoric to enjoin the felling of timber. Early in 1658, the town of Dorchester asserted that "timber and fire wood is of great use to the present and alsoe future generations and therefore [should] be prudently preserved from wracke" and destruction. But short-term practicality offers a more typical explanation of these restrictive measures.

Such prohibitions, of course, did not retard the subjugation of the New England forest. Since the economic controls usually lacked conservationist impulses, the authorities did not oppose the purposeful exploitation of the wilderness. . . .

The New England legislatures also expressed interest in appropriating the mineral wealth of the wilderness and urged the settlers to locate "mynes of mettalls and minerralls." Although the General Courts of Massachusetts and Connecticut retained the ultimate control of all mining operations in order to protect the general welfare, the colonial governments nevertheless offered bounties and partial monopolies "for the discovery of any mine." Periodically the New England colonies awarded land or other inducements to enterprising colonists for the extraction of mineral deposits. . . .

The settlers of New England diligently exploited the maritime wealth of their region. In the early years of settlement, the General Court permitted every householder to "have free fishing and fowling" provided that the separate towns had not established special restrictions. But within three decades of the founding of Massachusetts, the New England authorities responded to the pleas of the fishermen and prohibited the catching of certain fish during their spawning seasons. The destruction of these fish "at unseasonable times," they stated, "will in the issue tend to" spoil the trade. Economic motives, above all, determined the passage of such legislation, because the colonists generally overlooked the advantages of conservation. Governor Winthrop considered the migration of pigeons in 1648 "a great blessing, it being incredible what multitudes of them were killed daily." New Englanders also attempted to exterminate such common nuisances as wolves and foxes. And at mid-century, several towns offered bounties for black birds, jays, woodpeckers, and crows in order to protect the growing crops. Such measures reveal the colonists' short-sighted pragmatism in their endeavor to subjugate the wilderness.

As the settlers of New England successfully replenished the earth and exploited the natural resources of America, they commenced to praise not only the immediate products of their work, but also the transformation process itself. "What shall we say of the singular Providences of God," exclaimed Thomas Shepard and John Allin in the mid-1640s, "what shall wee say of the . . . Commonwealth erected in a Wildernesse, and in so few yeares brought" to such a state "that scarce the like can bee seen in any of our English Colonies in the richest places of this America, after many more yeares standing"? Writing a decade later, Edward Johnson extolled the transformation of "the close, clouded woods into goodly cornfields." "Wolves and Beares nurst up their young from the eyes of all behoulders," he declared, "in those very places where the streets are full of Girles and Boys sporting up and downe, with a continued concourse of people." In describing this metamorphosis, Johnson glorified the ceaseless task of subduing the earth. "[T]his remote, rocky, barren, bushy, wild-woody wilderness," he wrote, has "becom a second England for fertilness in so short a space, that it is indeed the wonder of the world." Although Johnson did not always endorse frontier expansion, he nevertheless recognized that such dispersal accelerated the transformation of the wilderness. "The constant penetrating farther into this Wilderness," he suggested, "hath caused the wild and uncouth woods to be fil'd with frequented wayes, and the large rivers to be overlaid with Bridges."

In subsequent years, New Englanders continued to praise the ongoing subjugation of the wilderness. John Norton admonished his congregation not to succumb to worldliness, but nevertheless declared with pride and wonder that "A spot of this vast *Jeshimon* [i.e., wilderness]" has been "converted into *Cornfields, Orchards, streets inhabited,* and a place of *Merchandize.*" John Higginson, in the Massachusetts Bay election sermon of 1663, similarly lauded the physical transformation in New England. "Look upon your townes and fields, look upon your habitations and shops and ships," he preached,"and behold your numerous posterity, and great encrease in the blessings of the Land and Sea." Michael Wigglesworth assured New Englanders that the Lord had turned "an howling wildernes . . . into a fruitful paradeis." And Nathaniel Saltonstall later explained the outbreak of the Indian War of 1675 in these terms. He maintained that King Philip, chief of the Wampanoag tribe, resented the occupation of his lands by the colonists, particularly after "seeing what Product the English have made of a Wilderness, through their Labour, and the Blessing of God thereon." Describing the forest in unsentimental language, these commentators applauded the constructive results of the cultivation of the wild lands of America.

As the settlers placed more and more land under the plough, they gradually perceived that New England and the wilderness were separate entities. . . . To the men of John Winthrop's generation, New England society in itself was a wilderness community. But as a result of physically transforming certain portions of the American forest, the colonists distinguished the cultivated acres from the remaining untrammeled areas with greater clarity. While they regarded the wilderness as the antithesis of civilization, the Puritans recognized that the emergence of habitable settlements constituted a permanent alteration of the American forest. Since they could now view New England as a distinct and unique place instead of as a vast wilderness with various theological attributes, the transformation of the forest accelerated the process of provincialization. For although the Puritans could reconcile the coexistence of wildness and civilization, they were clearly committed to civilization. The appearance of maturing towns thereby enabled New Englanders to focus their attention upon home lands instead of waste places.

These changes emerged in land surveys, travel reports, and natural descriptions. In the mid-1650s, several Massachusetts surveyors began to distinguish the wilderness lands from the virgin tracts they laid out. Thomas Danforth and Andrew Belchar surveyed a plot "surrounded with wildernes land," and other New Englanders often delineated boundaries with reference to "the wilderness land." In search of a suitable location for a plantation near Albany in 1672, John Paine implied that "the wildernes up the Rivor" varied measurably from the "valuable Landes" in the vicinity. Such descriptions reveal that New England and the wilderness were no longer synonymous terms and that the settlers qualitatively differentiated between the habitable areas and the unsubdued territories.

As ALAN TRACHTENBERG (b. 1932) demonstrates here, it is possible to write about a limited and specific subject and still draw conclusions of significance for the whole American experience. In this case the Brooklyn Bridge, connecting Long Island and Manhattan in metropolitan New York City, is the springboard from which Trachtenberg leaps to his important generalizations. The selection might serve as an introduction to the ideology which motivated the behavior Stewart Udall describes in the next essay.

Alan Trachtenberg

Progress and the Environment

At the Opening Ceremonies of Brooklyn Bridge on May 24, 1883, the Honorable Abram S. Hewitt began his oration with an image of primitive Manhattan.

Nature wore a hardy countenance, as wild and as untamed as the savage landholders. . . . The trees were lofty; and old, decayed and withered limbs contrasted with the younger growth of branches; and wild flowers wasted their sweetness among the dead leaves and uncut herbage at their roots. The wanton grape vine swung carelessly from the topmost boughs of the oak and the sycamore.

Here was the primal wilderness: the "fresh green breast of the new world" witnessed by Dutch sailors two hundred and seventy years before. Savage, rich, and going to waste — unrestrained nature had sole possession of the island.

The picture was affecting indeed, particularly side by side with "the panoramic view" that now "presents itself to the spectator standing upon the crowning arch of the Bridge":

In the place of stillness and solitude, the footsteps of these millions of human beings; instead of the smooth waters "unvexed by any keel," highways of commerce ablaze with the flags of all nations; and where once was the green monotony of forested hills, the piled and towering splendors of a vast metropolis, the countless homes of industry, the echoing marts of trade, the gorgeous palaces of luxury, the silent and steadfast spires of worship!

The first scene had been "the product of natural forces working through uncounted periods of time"; "patiently through ages," glaciers had carved a river between the two islands of "Manahatta" and "Seawanhaka" (Long Island). But the hand of man had "reversed" the "work of separation wrought so surely, yet so slowly, by the hand of Time"; the islands were "joined again, as once they were before the dawn of life in the far azoic ages." True, the wilderness was no more: the "green monotony" and "wanton grape vine" had given way before "piled and towered splendours." But was not this itself a fulfillment of man's "never-ending struggle . . . to subdue the forces of nature to his control and use?" The bridge was "not merely a creation," but a "growth": "It stands before us today as the sum and epitome of human knowledge; as the very heir of the ages."

Mr. Hewitt, a prominent Congressman, industrialist, and philanthropist, provided the fitting note for the occasion. Hailed as the Eighth Wonder of the world, the Great East River Bridge was tangible proof of America's achievement. Manhattan and Brooklyn were now major cities. And the country was united: more than a decade ago the railroad had reached the west coast. Now, wrote one observer, "with the completion of this bridge, the continent is entirely spanned, and one may visit, dry and shod and without the use of ferry boats, every city from the Atlantic to the Golden Gate." For many Americans in 1883, Brooklyn Bridge proved the nation to be healed of its wounds of civil war and again on its true course: the peaceful mastery of nature. The bridge seemed to embody those forces which had pruned the wild forest and set a city upon a hill. Economic necessity had led to the vast transportation developments in pre-Civil War America. Roads and canals, the paths of commerce, had followed the axe into the wilderness. But the economic motives of this exciting movement frequently lay

obscured beneath a rhetoric of myth. To many, roads fulfilled fervent dreams of the West as a new Garden of Eden, as the long-sought passage to the Orient. "Geographical predestination" was an argument as persuasive as the needs of commerce.

"Providence designed us to be a great and united nation," an orator had proclaimed in 1794, and geography was his proof: "Our lines are marked by the very hand of nature." It became clear, however, that the "hand of nature" created barriers as well as gateways to western expansion. The eastern mountain ranges and the many north-south rivers posed serious obstacles to communication. Moreover, the promising landscape raised a political doubt: could the republican principle, hitherto most successful in small nations, survive on so large a scale? Perhaps the very size of the continent would be the nation's undoing.

Transportation became the country's most urgent need. If geography bestowed a favor upon the young society, it also presented a challenge. In the early republic, the idea of "opening up" the West and binding it to the East became the focus of national unity. The high theme of "manifest destiny" required at first adequate roads. The verb used over and over again to express the idea of unity, "to cement the Union," was more than a figure of speech. Facing a landscape covered with barriers to its own promises, American society had to become technological in order to survive. It had to develop an industrial force in order to exploit the promise of the land.

Many Americans, however, had interpreted the promise of the land to be a great agrarian republic, spreading westward from the tide-lands. Jefferson envisioned such a republic, rooted in the soil, as America's best defense against the corruption of the Old World. Europe represented intrigue, superstition, crowded, fuming cities—evils America might avoid. The virgin land seemed to promise a new chance for man. As a republic of small, independent farms, America might escape the ravages of history. As long as the class of self-sufficient husbandmen predominated, Jefferson argued, the opportunity for liberation would remain. And separated from "the exterminating havoc of one quarter of the globe," the land itself encouraged optimism: "a chosen country, with room enough for our descendants to the hundredth and thousandth generation."

But to benefit from the land required an efficient system of communications. Thus, the building of roads and canals was to President Jefferson's mind one of the functions of the central government. Anticipating the liquidation of the public debt in 1806, Jefferson announced an ambitious program for the "progress of improvement." This program was to be, Henry Adams has pointed out, Jefferson's last bequest to mankind; it contained the crown of his hopes for republican government in America. The proposal was twofold, a national system of public higher education, and a national system of roads "commensurate with the majesty of the country." The roads would guarantee the Union: "New channels of communication will be opened between the States, the lines of separation will disappear, their interests will be identified, and their union cemented by new and indestructible ties." Jefferson's message of 1806 led to Secretary of the Treasury Albert Gallatin's *Report on Public Roads and Canals* (1808). Gallatin followed Jefferson in arguing that internal improvements should be federally controlled because their benefits were national:

Good roads and canals will shorten distances; facilitate commercial and personal intercourse; and unite, by a still more intimate community of interests, the most remote quarters of the United States. No other single operation within the power of government can more effectively tend to strengthen and perpetuate that union, which secures external independence, domestic peace, and internal liberty.

The main benefit was unity. In the Jeffersonian plan roads would protect the agrarian republic.

But improvements had ambiguous consequences. The first function of roads was to bring the farmer to market; hence they facilitated the commercial entanglements Jefferson hoped to avoid. In this alone, not to speak of the industrial plant necessary to construct them, roads threatened rather than protected agrarian self-sufficiency.

Alexander Hamilton, Jefferson's rival, recognized that internal improvements spelled the end of agrarianism; and as an advocate of manufacturing, he applauded this development. Roads and canals, he wrote in 1791, "put the remote parts of a country more nearly upon a level with those in the neighborhood of the town." For this reason, they are "the greatest of all improvements." The "cultivation of the remote" would equalize the level of civilization between town and country; it would produce a uniform society, devoted to industry rather than farming, to the town rather than the country. Productivity through the "application of ingenious machinery" to nature, not closeness to nature, would be the cardinal value.

In retrospect Hamilton appears to have been wiser than Jefferson; he stood on the side of historical inevitability. Jefferson had used the image of the "noble husbandman" to affirm the value of an organic way of life; but Hamilton foresaw that economic necessity would defeat this hope. What Jefferson affirmed lay beyond logic: it was a dream of timeless harmony with nature. Such a dream could hardly prevail against the dynamics of an expanding society.

Take, for example, the arguments of agrarians themselves. They supported Gallatin's program with considerable force. In 1810, a congressman from western New York, Peter B. Porter, spoke on the issue. In that year, he pointed out, more than a million farmers were scattered throughout the remote sections of New York, Pennsylvania, and Virginia. They were out of touch with the seaboard markets. Such isolation naturally caused hardships:

There is no place where the great staple articles for the use of civilized life can be produced in greater abundance with greater ease, and yet as respects most of the luxuries and many of the conveniences of life the people are poor.

The people are poor in luxuries and conveniences because "they have no vent for their produce at home." The lack of a market mocks the great fertility of the land.

Such is the fertility of their land that one-half of their time spent in labor is sufficient to produce every article which their farms are capable of yielding, in sufficient quantities for their own consumption, and there is nothing to incite them to produce more.

These farmers, it is clear, wanted no part of self-sufficiency; they apparently preferred agrarian business to agrarian independence. They judged the value of the land by how quickly they could convert its products into cash.

And roads were to lead away from the land more often than to it. An effective argument for persuading farmers to support local improvement projects was that construction would inflate the cash value of nearby lands. Land values rather than the land itself seemed to keep Americans on the go in this pre-Civil War period. A new land bubble further west might make one's fortune. Roads were a good investment; they offered a double opportunity, a fast killing and a fast get-away. Not the old homestead but modern capitalism lay at the end of the line.

It is well known that American society followed Hamilton's course toward manufacturing and capitalism. But Jefferson's dream did not die; in fact, the rapid movement toward cities and bigness contributed as much as any intrinsic force in the dream itself to keep it alive. As Leo Marx has so forcefully shown, the pastoral ideal persisted as a reaction — unconscious as well as calculated — to what Carlyle in 1831 called "industrialism." In particular, while industrialism was transforming America into a land of cities and railroads, some Americans continued to celebrate the road in the language of the Jeffersonian utopia.

[They] seemed not to concede that a basic conflict between two ways of life was at stake in the massive transformation of nature.... Ralph Waldo Emerson, for example, in a lecture "The Young American" (1844), saw internal improvements as "beneficent for America"; they eliminate "local peculiarities and hostilities," and reveal a "sublime and friendly Destiny." Most of all, he found, the railroad carries city people into the country and introduces them to the land. The railroad might even plant a garden in the West; he calls it a "magician's rod, in its power to evoke the sleeping energies of land and water." Emerson, like most of his contemporaries, expected the machine to serve what was still basically an agrarian society.

Thomas Ewbank had no such illusions. At one time a manufacturer, Ewbank was

Commissioner of Patents in the 1840's. In his Report of 1849 he spread before Congress the prospect of "an infinity of work" for Americans. Man's original sin, he wrote, was indolence, not disobedience. But shirk it as he will, man's work will not be finished until "the planet is wholly changed from its natural wilderness . . . into a fit theatre for cultivated intelligences." Until then, all other activities were pointless; technology provided all the poetry and morality man needed. A steamer, he wrote, was a mightier epic than the *Iliad,* and "a lever, hammer, pulley, wedge, and screw, are actual representations of great natural truth." Ewbank foresaw endless progress through machinery. Engineers and inventors held "the future destinies of the planet in their hands."

Ewbank's ideas were an outgrowth of eighteenth-century empiricism and deism. He saw the world as an immense mechanism. In *The World a Workshop* (1855), Ewbank claimed that the inventor is the true man; to be human is to be a "Manipulator of Matter." In regard to agrarianism, Ewbank echoed Hamilton: "the hypothesis that the chief employment of man was to till the soil and raise cattle, is an unworthy one." Food, he argued, is a mere adjunct to life; agrarians are "surface dreamers." He did not want a reconciliation between agrarianism and industrialism, but a total surrender to the machine. This, he saw, would establish a new way of life, a way of rapid transportation, cities, and capitalism. . . .

The dream of a tenderly cultivated plot has consistently appealed to Americans, perhaps never more so than now, in an age of automation. But strong as that appeal has been, American behavior toward the land has been something else again. Americans have always subscribed to Eden, and proceeded to transform it in the name of progress. This was true even before modern mechanical devices. It was true from the very beginning, when the sight of untamed wilderness going to waste converted transplanted Europeans into Americans. Francis Grund, an Austrian traveler, observed in 1837 that Americans had always

treated nature as a conquered subject: not as a mother who gave them birth. They were the children of another world, who came to burn, ransack and destroy, and not to preserve what they had found. They burned the forests, dug up the bowels of the earth, diverted rivers from their course, or united them at their pleasure; and annihilated the distances which separated the North from the South, and the East from the West.

Americans were such excellent transformers of nature, Grund wrote, that no single change seemed permanent; they "live in the future, and *make* their country as they go on." To many Americans, the going itself was the main business of man on a wild continent beyond the reach of history. Jefferson's hopes for local attachments to the soil were defeated by the very means necessary to open the continent, the means of transportation. Not the land, not the garden, but the road, from Jefferson's own national turnpike to the latest superhighway, has expressed the essential way of American life.*

---

*I mean, of course, not only the literal road—but all that is implied by it: cities, automobiles and the power of the automobile industry, construction companies—and boondoggles. In other words, an entire social order which values "quick turnover" above planning and harmony.

As Secretary of the Interior under Presidents John F. Kennedy and Lyndon B. Johnson, STEWART L. UDALL (b. 1920) occupied an advantageous position for understanding American environmental history. A native of Arizona and a descendant of the Mormon pioneer John D. Lee, Udall has nonetheless been able to shake free from the pioneer perspective far enough to criticize it vigorously. His essay raises an important problem: can we charge the pioneers with environmental irresponsibility? Or were their actions entirely appropriate to the time and place in which they lived? If the sky was dark with passenger pigeons and the hills covered with virgin timber, what would you have done? Perhaps the severest criticism should be reserved for those who have carried the pioneer attitudes towards the environment into a frontierless age.

Stewart L. Udall

The Raid on Resources

The Big Raid on resources began, in a sense, with mountain men and their beaver traps, and reached a series of high points in the last decades of the nineteenth century. Its first phase involved only the harm caused by primitive tools, but the second was linked to the machines of the industrial revolution, which made possible large-scale harvesting of re-sources—and large-scale land damage.

It was the intoxicating profusion of the American continent which induced a state of mind that made waste and plunder inevitable. A temperate continent, rich in soils and minerals and forests and wildlife, enticed men to think in terms of infinity rather than facts, and produced an overriding fallacy that was nearly our undoing—the Myth of Superabundance. According to the myth, our resources were inexhaustible. It was an assumption that made wise management of the land and provident husbandry super-fluous.

A growing nation needed wood for housing and fuel and shipbuilding, and the biggest of the Big Raids began in the woods. The virgin forests of North America were among the masterpieces of the natural world: east of the Great Plains nearly every acre was covered by trees; to the west softwood stands flourished on the slopes and in the valleys of the Rocky Mountains; and rising above the

Pacific shore line, in the most productive timber zone in the world, redwood and fir stands provided a crescendo of arboreal splendor.

Europe had hardly a dozen tree types. The American expanse had more than a hundred, and our many soils and climate zones produced the largest and oldest trees, and the most accessible commercial stocks on any continent. The first task of forest-bound colonists was to develop woodsmanship: homes and stockades had to be roughhewn, land cleared, and firewood cut. Farming awaited the work of the broadax: clearings could be carved out of the virgin thickets only through great effort or by the deliberate use of fire.

Tree cutters were the advance men of agrarianism, and the worst acts of forest destruction were oftentimes explained away with the carefree rationalization that such devastation was necessary to "let daylight into the swamps." The common assumption was that trees, like Indians, were an obstacle to settlement, and the woodsmen were therefore pioneers of progress.

Until the machines came along, the Ax Age American and the Stone Age Indian could inflict only limited damage. Small local sawmills provided all the finished lumber needed in the early days, and it was about 1800 before cities required lumber in wholesale lots, and enterprisers learned to organize machines and men to produce it. Then came the circular saw and the steam mill. The wood-pulp process for making paper was invented, and a frantic wood rush began that would strip most of our forests and help puncture the Myth of Superabundance. The sad truth is that when the big lumber raids got under way, our thinking on forests was fixed, and we regarded those who invaded the forest heartlands as the leaders of the westward advance.

Lumbering quickly became our largest manufacturing industry. Conditions could not have been more favorable: timberland was cheap, labor was cheap, and a small investment would outfit a mill and start a log boom. The onslaught began in New England, moved across New York and Pennsylvania, leveled the vast pineries of the Lake states, and finally cut a wide swath through the yellowpine stands of the South and the West. Until 1909, the year output reached its peak, production continued to increase in crazy cycles of boom and bust. There was enough wood for a thousand years, the optimists said, but the lumbermen leveled most of the forests in a hundred.

The devastation was not caused by logging alone: careless loggers caused fires that burned as much as 25,000,000 acres each year. Some irresponsible lumbermen deliberately set fire to the debris they left behind, thus destroying seedlings that would have replenished the ravaged forests.

The average life of a sawmill was the twenty years it took to strip a hinterland. As this brawling industry ran its course, such towns as Bangor, Albany, Williamsport, Saginaw, Muskegon, Eureka, and Portland in succession briefly boasted the title "lumber capital of the world."

Lumbering, in its raider phase, was a strip-and-run business: the waste of wood was enormous, and when the best stands had been cut, the operator dismantled his mill and moved it farther west, letting the raped land go back into public ownership because the taxes went unpaid. In some areas sawmill ghost towns still clutter the landscape. Trees, like gold or silver, were "mined," for the land-skinners wanted the quickest profits the system would allow.

It was an era, too, of human heroics, and the Paul Bunyan loggers and lumberjacks who took on and tamed the howling wilderness had a prowess that still commands our respect. Their feats of main strength, however, somehow symbolized the mindless, planless approach that ruined vast sections of our land.

The destruction of the American forests was facilitated by the Great Giveaway of land, which made the raids possible; by the optimism of the people, which made the Great Giveaway plausible as a policy; and by the political power of the raider captains themselves, which kept exploitation going full tilt once the harvest began.

Many of the states outdid the federal government in "giving away" timberland. Maine and Pennsylvania sold off enormous tracts for twelve and one-half cents an acre. North Carolina, not to be outdone, auctioned off choice hardwood stands for ten cents. Some of the best federal timberlands were also put on the market at bargain prices. "Sell cheap" was our slogan, and leaders like President Andrew Jackson and John C. Calhoun wanted to cede all federal land to the states free of charge and be done with national trusteeship.

For shrewd lumbermen, however, there were ways to take trees without buying huge tracts of land. A common practice was to purchase adjacent forty-acre pieces of public land and cut all around them. The "round-forty" was the classic joke of the lumber industry.

A few provident grants were made, but "giveaway" was the rule, and prodigality reached its peak between 1850 and 1871 when an area larger than France, England, Scotland, and Wales was granted to the railroad companies. The loose forest "homestead" laws passed by Congress in the 70's and 80's prompted the forest historian, Samuel Trask Dana, to conclude that by 1885 "ninety percent of the entries under the Timber Culture Acts were fraudulent."

The politics-ridden General Land Office was given neither the men nor money needed to manage the land, or to enforce the law. In any event, there was no public opinion to support action against timber thieves and trespassers—who were, more often than not, regarded as upstanding citizens. Referring to timber depredations in his 1870 official report, one high Washington official argued that the whole public domain should be disposed of: "The entire standing army of the United States could not enforce the regulations," he said. "The remedy is to sell the lands."

Timber was not the only resource plundered by the raiders. The soil that had been eons in the making was devastated in some regions as thoroughly as were the forests.

In 1852, Anthony Chabot, a California gold miner, ingeniously devised a canvas hose and nozzle that would wash banks of gold-bearing gravel into placer pits for processing. Chabot's labor-saving short cut caught on in the Mother Lode country above Sacramento, and by 1870 his crude hose had evolved into the "Little Giant," a huge nozzle that could tear up whole hillsides.

The result of the hydraulic mining was the massive movement of soil into the rivers that drained the Sierra Nevada. For every ounce of gold collected, tons of topsoil and gravel were washed into the river courses below. With the spring floods, clear streams became a chaos of debris, rocks, and silt; communities downstream were inundated with muck, and fertile bottomlands were blanketed with mud and gravel. The town of Marysville, along the Yuba River, was forced to build ever-larger levees that rose higher than the city's rooftops. In 1875, a big storm sent the Yuba over the levees and filled the city with silt.

The townsmen and farmers who suffered damage protested, but they got no-where. Gold was California's first in-dustry, and by the standards of the times, the hydraulic miners had as much right to slice off the hills as the farmers had to cultivate the valleys below. Minerals are not a renewable resource, and the land legacy of any mining operation is, neces-sarily, a pit, a shaft, or a hole. However, in their reckless effort to extract gold, the hydraulic miners asserted the right to damage other resources irreparably—and the homes of other citizens as well. In the 1870's, the right of each individual to do as he pleased was sacrosanct. The miners had enough friends in Sacramento to enable them to continue their onslaught on the mountainsides until the devasta-tion forced the California legislature, in 1884, to outlaw hydraulic mining alto-gether.

Like the raids on lumber and gold, the raid on oil and natural gas was a strip-and-run business, with enormous in-cidental waste. When one field was depleted, the oilmen moved on to an-other. Where one well might have suf-ficed to drain an underground reservoir, there were often fifteen or twenty.

The big oil strikes began in the 1860's and, as with lumber, a succession of towns across America boasted, for a time, the title of "Oil Capital of the World"—Titus-ville, Pithole, Oil City, and Bradford in the Appalachian area; Tulsa and Okla-homa City in mid-continent; Kilgore in Texas; Los Angeles in California.

When oil came, it was usually in gush-ers that spewed the black liquid across the landscape with volcanic force. In the first big oil boom in Pennsylvania, just after the Civil War, gushers wasted oil at the rate of 3,000 barrels a day. But that record was soon broken and, in 1901, Spindletop in Texas flowed wild for nine days at the rate of 110,000 barrels a day before it was brought under control. The

gushers went uncontrolled because early oilmen did not understand geology. Gushers caught fire, oil was allowed to evaporate in earthen dams, or to escape down creeks and gullies in an orgy of waste.

When early disputes arose as to owner-ship, the courts held that the oil belonged to anyone who could capture it. This Law of Capture put a premium on speed, and most of the time the big rewards went to whoever struck the underground treasure first. Consequently, operators who wanted to conserve supplies were forced to com-pete with greedy and shortsighted men.

Of all the waste associated with petro-leum, perhaps none was so great as the waste of natural gas. The oil producer, not realizing that gas energy brought oil to the surface, allowed it to dissipate.

When it came to petroleum, the Myth of Superabundance reached an absurd climax. It was widely believed that oil was continuously being formed in the earth and was thus, like every other re-source, supposedly inexhaustible.

A similar lack of land insight was re-sponsible for the worst shortcoming of our stewardship, the appalling erosion of topsoil. Some of our farmers and stock-men knew what they wanted, but they knew too little about the delicate balances of nature. For example, deterioration of the Western grasslands by overgrazing was usually a slow process. It was hard for a rancher to notice each spring that the grass on his range grew a little thinner, and that, as the years passed, the invasion of weeds expanded. But as the overgraz-ing continued, scrub growth took over, the slopes began to wash, small gullies developed into large ones, and ranchers found themselves the proprietors of homemade badlands.

The farmers who tried to raise crops in the grassland country ran into similar trouble. Many regions west of the 100th meridian should never have been plowed at all: the familiar pattern of farming in the East was out of place in a region of little rain. In this country of half-steppe, half-desert, the soil was anchored to the land by grass. Once the plains were plowed, the dry, upturned soil had no protection against the driving winds. In most areas the soil might have been saved if the farmers had planted cover crops or had limited their plowing to the lands they intended to farm intensively. They failed to realize, however, that drought was a recurrent fact of life on the Great Plains, and when the dry years came, crops withered, the dust deepened, and whistling winds lifted thousands of tons of topsoil into the atmosphere.

The farmers' failure was a failure to grasp elementary earth facts. Like tobacco and cotton farmers of the South, they abused the land because they were ignorant of its laws of self-renewal. Aldo Leopold, who later looked with a scientist's eye on the prairie country, saw the subtle interrelations the settlers had missed:

The black prairie was built by the prairie plants, a hundred distinctive species of grasses, herbs and shrubs; by the prairie fungi, insects, and bacteria; by the prairie mammals and birds, all interlocked in one humming community of cooperations and competitions, one biota. This biota, through ten thousand years of living and dying, burning and growing, preying and fleeing, freezing and thawing, built that dark and bloody ground we call prairie.

Defeated by dust storms of their own making, thousands of farm families packed up their belongings and retreated eastward. On the Great Plains, from the 1880's on, the tides of migration rolled back and forth with the weather. After each rainy cycle of sod-busting, the dusty land waited for the wind. The settlers

thus set the stage for the Dust Bowl of the 1930's—the most tragic land calamity ever to strike the North American continent.

In the long run overgrazing and over-farming proved as disastrous as over-mining and overlogging. Yet the raids on resources were not limited to soil or gold or timber. They extended to biological resources as well. The Big Raid on wildlife began when the *voyageurs* and the colonists found that pelts woult fetch a good price in European markets. It entered its final phase when the first major expedition of mountain men went up the Missouri to trap beaver. Within a decade, John Jacob Astor's American Fur Company with its competitors could ship pelts by the hundreds of thousands to Europe, where they were converted into men's high hats.

The trappers who were making a livelihood and the organizers like Astor who were making fortunes from beaver failed to realize that they were destroying a species. Owing to a happy accident, however, the beaver raid stopped short of extermination—the beaver hat went out of style by 1840 and the beaver was saved.

The shifting fashions were not so kind to another aquatic mammal, the fur seal of the North Pacific Ocean. In the late eighteenth century, seamen had often observed the northward migrations of enormous seal herds. In 1786, a Russian navigator, Gerasim Pribilof, gazed in unbelief at some volcanic islands in the Bering Sea where millions of seals blackened the shore lines. The enterprising Russian planted a colony on one of the lonely islands and piled his ship high with pelts. For eighty years Russian ships raided the fabulous rookeries of the Pribilof Islands. When the Czar agreed to sell Alaska to the United States for $7,200,000 in 1866, the seal population, estimated originally at 5,000,000 had been cut in half.

The Americans of the Alaska Commercial Company, which received the United States franchise for the Pribilof furs, proceeded to outdo the Russians in slaughtering the animals. They launched a promotional sales campaign that soon brought competitors into the Bering Sea —seagoing hunters who shot the animals in the ocean during their migrations.

As the Pacific whaling industry declined, whalers turned to sealing, and by 1880 seal hunting on the high seas was a big business. Most of the animals which were shot were gravid, and many were not recovered; as a result, the waste was enormous.

The United States government showed less interest in the depletion of the herds than in the revenues paid by the sealers. In the first twenty years of its operation the Alaska Company took enough sealskins to repay the entire cost of the Alaska Purchase. By 1911, when the Fur Seal Treaty with Canada, Japan, and Russia was finally approved, only 3 per cent of the original seal population remained. If the treaty had been delayed another few years, the fur seal might well have become the first major marine victim of the Myth of Superabundance.

Of all wildlife species on the continent the most numerous was the passenger pigeon. At the beginning of the nineteenth century the number of these birds was estimated to be an incredible 5,000,000,000. Around 1810, Ornithologist Alexander Wilson reported sighting in Kentucky a single flock which was a mile wide and 240 miles long, containing, he guessed, more than 2,000,000,000 birds. It is likely that these prolific pigeons then constituted about a third of the entire bird population of the United States.

Succulent and easy to kill, they were shipped by the carload to city markets, and some farmers used them for hog feed. It was inevitable that these vast flocks would be depleted. They were an easy mark for the hunters, and the forest levelers were destroying their habitat. Ultimately, however, the passenger pigeons were not depleted—they were exterminated. At the end of the nineteenth century there was not one to be seen, and a few years later the last survivor of the species died in the Cincinnati zoo.

A good many other species of edible wild birds—robins, blackbirds, sparrows, thrushes—were in similar danger until the Audubon Societies and their allies took up cudgels for their protection. Some of the big birds whose bright plumage was much in demand for ladies' hats— the kingfishers, terns, eagles, pelicans, egrets, and herons—also came close to the abyss of extinction.

Many other native species barely survived the onslaught of the Big Raids. The sea otter was pursued to near extinction by rapacious seal hunters; the salmon runs were eliminated on nearly all New England rivers by mill dams and pollution; the whales were hunted relentlessly until commercial whale oil was replaced by petroleum.

That massive emblem of the American frontier, the buffalo—our largest and most valuable wildlife resource—was nearly extinguished in an unprecedented campaign of animal butchery. No one knows how many buffalo there were when Jefferson's Louisiana Purchase made their ranges part of our public domain. Informed guesses extend from 10,000,000 to 100,000,000, but whatever the exact number, they were the wildlife wonder of our continent.

The size of the buffalo herds was a source of awe to the plainsmen, and

Colonel R. I. Dodge once wrote of a herd he saw in Arkansas in the early 70's: "From the top of Pawnee Rocks I could see from six to ten miles in almost every direction. This whole vast space was covered with buffalo, looking at a distance like a compact mass."

The big kill began when the Civil War ended. The army wanted the animals killed in order to starve out the Plains Indians; the cattlemen wanted them killed to save forage for their own livestock; the railroad men wanted them killed to supply profitable freight in the form of hides; the market hunters wanted to kill them for their tongues and hides; and sportsmen came to kill them for trophies and for pleasure. For a few years buffalo hunting was the main, grisly business of the Plains country, and the more flamboyant of the market hunters—men like Bill Cody and Wild Bill Hickok—romanticized the last, gory raids and capitalized on their acclaim long after the great herds were gone.

The hunters roamed the bison ranges with specially designed rifles which could drop a buffalo on a far hillside. If the wind was right and if luck held, the hunters found a herd and picked off dozens of animals before the rest panicked. The westward push of the railroads was a boon to the hunters, and the organized slaughter began in earnest when the tracks reached the Plains. A good hunter could bring in more than 1,000 hides a year, but the venison—more succulent by far than the steak of a longhorn steer—was left for the wolves and vultures. An estimated 1,000,000 buffalo were killed each year from 1872 to 1875. At Forth Worth, hides awaiting shipment were stacked in high rows over a quarter-mile long.

As the massacre continued, there was concern in some quarters that these shaggy symbols of the Wild West would be completely annihilated. But General Phil Sheridan boasted that the buffalo hunters were doing more to subjugate the Plains Indians than the army had been able to do in thirty years. In scorched-earth language the general advised the Texas legislature: "Let them kill, skin and sell until the buffalo is exterminated, as it is the only way to bring about lasting peace and allow civilization to advance." For the same reasons, in 1875, President Grant vetoed a buffalo-protection bill, the first measure ever passed by the Congress of the United States to protect a species of wildlife.

Within five years the Southern herds had been wiped out, and the buffalo hunters turned their attention northward. In the fall of 1883 a hunting party came upon a group of 10,000 of the animals near the Cannon Ball River in North Dakota. By November this herd had been finished off, and the hunters gathered up their hides and retired for the winter. The following spring the Indians and white hunters waited for the annual migration to begin, but they had done their work too well. Only a few hundred scattered survivors could be found. The raid on the buffalo was over.

Back as far as the 1830's, artist George Catlin had suggested that large areas should be set aside for the buffalo—and the Indians—as a great outdoor museum of natural history. If his advice had been followed, more than the buffalo might have been saved: it is ironical that the very grasslands that were the natural home of these magnificent beasts later became the scene of the overgrazing and overfarming that caused the dust bowl.

Entwined with the tragedy of the buffalo was the tragedy of human blindness that depicted the national mood. Only a handful of men spoke up to protest the slaughter, and, worse, the trustee of all the people, President Ulysses S. Grant, cast his lot with waste and butchery. In an era of superabundance and government inaction, public resources owned by everyone were, in practice, the responsibility of no one. By a fortunate accident some remnant herds in Yellowstone and in Canada were overlooked by the hunters. Their descendants that remain today on a few Western wildlife refuges are a vivid symbol of the most savage hour in the rape of American resources.

Most of the raids on wildlife, like those on other resources, were carried out in a devil-take-the-hindmost spirit under the deadly assumption that the supply was unending. No matter how many buffalo were shot, there would always be more. Bemused by the Myth of Superabundance, Americans ignored the elementary laws of nature. They realized too late that the Atlantic salmon would never come leaping up the rivers again, the sky would never again be filled with passenger pigeons, and the buffalo would no longer make men pause in awe at the thunder of their passing.

The brand of extreme individualism that necessarily characterized the frontier dominated our attitudes toward all resources during the nineteenth century. The intentions of those who launched the assault on our land were, however, as diverse as the American way of life itself.

Some who unwittingly diminished the productivity of our land were not raiders at all, but imprudent husbandmen like the early tobacco and cotton farmers who "wore out" two or three farms in a futile and halfhearted search for the secrets of soil fertility. The homesteaders and their sons who plowed up the Dust Bowl were honest husbandmen who never understood the Draconian laws of drought and the importance of grass cover in an arid land. The buffalo hunters, by contrast, realized full well that they were liquidating a resource, but considered themselves patriotic outriders of the civilized advance.

There were others, however, who found themselves caught up in a greedy game in which success went to those who cut the most corners and got to the most valuable resources first. The winners of these ruthless races were acquainted with hard work and sharp practice. They were men of pitiless initiative, with a total indifference to the needs of future generations. The most destructive of all the raiders were the hydraulic miners and the loggers who set fire to the large areas they had stripped: their wastelands and "barrens" stand today as monuments to a form of *laissez-faire* individualism that ignored sound husbandry.

This reckless era was also the time when Manifest Destiny came to full flower and we completed the settlement of the frontier. It had episodes of heroism and colonizing and empire building, but it should not be forgotten that it was also the period when we raided the Indians, raided the continent—and raided the future.

A European and a curator of art, HANS HUTH (b. 1892) brings a novel but highly appropriate point of view to his subject. The nineteenth-century Americans he discusses made so bold as to suggest that growth and quantity were not the only criteria for progress and happiness. The *kind* of life lived amid abundance, they implied, also deserved recognition and sometimes, as in the case of parks, demanded that limits be set on the expansion of civilization. Huth's *Nature and the American: Three Centuries of Changing Attitude* is a standard source of the history of American attitude and action toward the environment. Be sure to notice the several points on which Huth's Americans and those described by Carroll, Trachtenberg, and Udall differ radically. How would you account for the difference?

Hans Huth

The Aesthetic Emphasis

What was the attitude of the colonials toward nature, and how did it develop later?. . . The pioneers' point of view . . . rejected in nature that which was not of immediate and practical use. . . .

To traveler and settler alike, nature seemed uncouth in the extreme, and they felt that they were in a "most howling wilderness amidst wild men and beasts." Toward the beginning of the eighteenth century there were occasional changes in this attitude, even in the core of Puritan stock. For example, Jonathan Edwards, the Connecticut minister, who was dismissed from his pulpit for his too strict adherence to the Puritan dogma, rather freely expressed his deep love for the beauties of nature which he considered an emanation of the Son of God. "We behold the fragrant rose and lily . . . the easiness and naturalness of trees and rivers are shadows of His beauty . . . the golden edges of an evening cloud . . . the blue sky . . . the ragged rocks . . . and the brows of mountains." While such sentiments apparently were admitted in disguised form, a New Englander ordinarily would have frowned on the enjoyment of nature as a pastime, since it would have been neither "useful" nor "innocent," but plain wasteful, and therefore vicious and leading to excess and sin. Southerners, of course, were more tolerant, but still contemplations of nature were rare before 1750. . . .

Only in the second half of the eigh-

From Hans Huth, "Yosemite: The Story of an Idea," *Sierra Club Bulletin* (1948), pp. 48–53, 57–59, 61–66, 68, 71–72. Footnotes omitted.

teenth century did writers express more clearly defined thoughts about their relations with nature. . . . William Bartram, Hector St. Jean de Crèvecoeur, Alexander Wilson, and Philip Freneau all came into close contact with nature by profession as well as by avocation, and all of them were conscious of the newness of their adventure on being confronted with virgin woods, savannahs, and lakes, not previously charted by white men. They as well as their readers had been prepared for their fresh experience by the works of English deists, such as Lord Shaftesbury, who had shaped their minds to perceive the possibility of a new kind of relationship between man and nature. At the same time they became acquainted with critics of the type of Edward Burke, whose recognition that a quality like "sublimity" should be coordinated with the beautiful, laid the foundation for a new aesthetic doctrine which was immediately taken up and applied. A little later the English Reverend William Gilpin became known as the erudite who had spent years in search and description of the "Picturesque." Scarcely any writer on "nature" in the beginning of the nineteenth century failed to follow him and use his vocabulary. Only after the integration of such new definitions were writers properly equipped to furnish more unconventional and precise appraisals of nature. Imbued with this new spirit, William Bartram, 1739–1823, traveling between 1773 and 1777, asked his countrymen to behold "as yet unmodified by the hand of man . . . the unlimited variety and truly astonishing scenes of landscape and perspective.". . .

In Alexander Wilson's (1766–1813) epic poem, "The Foresters, Descriptive of a Pedestrian Tour to the Niagara," even the title reveals an attitude toward the natural wonders of this country. The poem is not well remembered now and probably was never very popular. But Wilson himself, wandering up and down the seaboard states and penetrating into remote places to peddle subscriptions to his bird publications, was a well-known figure and a most eloquent advocate in the propagation of love for and interest in the beauties of nature. In his time the public knew Wilson far better than they did his competitor, [John James] Audubon, who came into public view and gained a certain popularity much later.

Among the scores of travelers who roamed through the country for various purposes, it is easy to pick out some who took real interest in the scenes with which they were confronted. . . . To visitors beholding Natural Bridge in Virginia for the first time, it is, according to Thomas Jefferson, impossible for their emotions "arising from the sublime to be felt beyond what they are here . . . the rapture of the spectator is really indescribable." To understand this praise we must realize that Natural Bridge was one of those objects to which a "curio" value had attached. The appreciation of this value, which has nothing to do with the aesthetic or sentimental merit of an object, was one of long standing. It had interested travelers the world over, ever since they had first set out on pilgrimages. Trenton Falls, Mammoth Cave, and, of course, Niagara Falls were some of the other places in this country regarded as "curious" and "landmarks," to be seen by every foreign traveler. So in evaluating the "raptures" of travelers, we must be careful to distinguish mere delight in a curio value from the growing appreciation of scenic qualities of nature. In the travel accounts of Timothy Dwight, president of Yale in 1795, we are immediately reassured that the joy he expressed in the sights he beheld was genuine. An untiring traveler of the American country-side, he wandered "with emotions, similar to those with which, when a child, he roamed through the wilderness."

Evaluation of the attitudes toward nature of writers of the early nineteenth century is difficult only because it becomes hard to know whom to select among the many who were taking an increasing interest in the American scene. Above all is of course James Fenimore Cooper, whose *Pioneers** must be regarded as one of the most significant books in this respect. Here is one of its typical passages in which Natty Bumpo expresses his feelings:

..."when I felt lonesome ... I would go into the Catskills and spend a few days on that hill ..." "What see you when you get there?" asked Edwards ... "Creation, lad, all creation," said Natty. "How should a man who has lived in towns ... know anything about the wonders of the woods? ... None know how often the hand of God is seen in the wilderness, but them that rove it for a man's life."

A study of William Cullen Bryant's (1794–1878) poems will clearly prove that devotion to nature was one of his outstanding characteristics. This devotion is early expressed in "Thanatopsis," and it is later confirmed by James Russell Lowell who hailed the dean of American poets on his seventieth birthday:

The voice of the hills did his obey;
The torrents flashed and trembled in his
  song;
He brought our native fields from far
  away ...

While much interest has been shown lately in Thomas Cole's painting (1801–1848), some attention should also be given to his journals for their warmhearted

descriptions of the "sublimity of untamed wilderness, and majesty of the eternal mountains." But Cole did not confide his thoughts only to his journal; we know at least of one lecture on "American Scenery," which he gave in 1835 before the New York Lyceum. Though we do not know the contents of this paper, we can well imagine how Cole talked about "primeval forests, virgin lakes and waterfalls," feasting his eye and being hallowed "to his soul by their freshness from the creation."

Another romantic writer was Charles Fenno Hoffmann (1806–1884), the first editor of *Knickerbocker Magazine.* In 1834 he set out all alone to travel west on horseback. He too was enchanted by the beauty nature had lavished on the country and asked, "Why are there none to sing her primeval glories in our land? More important, however, was George Catlin (1796–1872), another untiring explorer and painter, whose particular interest lay in the "looks and customs of the vanishing races of native man in America." Traveling up the Missouri River into the heart of the Indian country (1832), Catlin beheld the vast forest covering the banks of the river and he, perhaps as the first man in this country to do so, had the imagination to conceive the idea that these realms "might in future be seen (by some great protecting policy of government) preserved in their pristine beauty and wildness, in a *magnificent park,* where the world could see for ages to come, the native Indian in his classic attire, galloping his wild horse ... amid the fleeting herds of elks and buffaloes. What a beautiful and thrilling specimen for America to preserve and hold up to the view of her refined citizens and the world, in future ages! A *nation's Park,* containing man and beast, in all the wild and freshness of their nature's beauty." This passage was

---

*The book was published in 1823.–Ed.

first published in one of the letters Catlin sent to the *New York Daily Commercial Advertiser* in 1833 from the Indian Territory. Thus was planted the seed of an idea which, although it took more than three decades to develop, was immediately well circulated in the widely read New York newspaper.

Henry Thoreau's *Walden* and the thirty volumes of his journal dedicated to recording observations on nature should be enough to show his interest in our problem. In one of his most pertinent passages he wrote:

Why should not we ... have our national preserves ... in which the bear and panther, and some even of the hunter race, may still exist, and not be "civilized off the face of the earth"... for inspiration and our true recreation? Or should we, like villains, grub them all up for poaching on our own national domains?

Of Emerson's many statements concerning either his appreciation or his deep understanding of nature and the intrinsic qualities of his native soil, one might quote a remark he made in his Boston lecture about "The Young American" (1844) as reported in the *Dial*: "The interminable forests should become graceful parks, for use and delight." This passage, deleted in later book versions, seems to be the one publicly pronounced which follows Catlin's postulate of 1833 most closely. Cole took up the same idea by stating that "Americans have a strong desire for excellence ... a love of nature ... one cause of it—the wilderness passing away and the necessity of saving and perpetuating its features." All these remarks show that by the middle of the century, growing numbers of people not only had begun to take interest in the outdoors but also had realized that conservation measures were becoming necessary. . . .

One of the reasons for this change was that traveling along the seaboard states had become easier. As long as the roads had been the main lines of transportation, traveling had been difficult, since horseback riding was not suitable for pleasure trips. . . . Only great people owned carriages; stages were ridden only when they had to be, since they were uncomfortable and roads—even the national roads— were in hideous shape. With the opening of the Erie Canal in 1827, traveling began to be thought of as a pleasure. Canal boats, moving four miles an hour and offering fair sleeping and dining facilities, made trips which were called the "Grand Tour," up through New York State to Lake Ontario, where passengers could visit Niagara Falls conveniently. What a thrilling experience it must have been to sail through the new and thriving cities of Utica, Palmyra, and Rochester—and just outside town to enjoy "unbroken wildness"! In his essays and novels published after the early 'thirties, N. P. Willis, the fashionable chronicler of his day, described how tourists swarming around Lake George and along the St. Lawrence were eager to discover the "unhackneyed" beauties of silent lakes and vast forests. . . . The constantly increasing love of the out-of-doors caused many city dwellers who could afford it to take up summer residence in suburbs or even in the country and along the Hudson and Schuylkill.". . .

With the expansion of railroads in the 'thirties, traveling in some respects was made easier than in the heyday of the canal boats. *Davison*, the standard traveling guide for the Atlantic states, many times reprinted between 1822 and 1840, informs us that "the recent and gigantic internal improvements in the northern and middle states, and the development of new and highly interesting natural scenery, together with the increased facilities for travelling," greatly augmented the number of tourists who undertook "what has been usually denominated the Fashionable or Northern Tour." Although trains, with their speed of two and three miles an hour, did not travel any more rapidly than canal boats, such distant regions as the White Mountains now became more easily accessible. . . .

The vanguard of tourists to the West was formed by artists, and John Banvard was one of the pioneers. He had traveled down the whole course of the Mississippi in 1840 and had painted scenes along the banks of the river on a canvas of enormous length especially woven for him at Lowell. Later, turning his flatboat into a show boat and floating down the Wabash, he exhibited his panorama to four thousand paying visitors—an audience which at this date was probably interested primarily in beholding the American scene in a comfortable manner. Other artists managed to go west by traveling with surveying parties. Albert Bierstadt went along with General F. W. Landers' expedition which mapped the railroad route across the Platte River and through Wyoming to the Pacific. Bierstadt, on his return, was the first to show the East a representative picture of the Rocky Mountains. When in 1857 he made his first trip to California, he became greatly interested in the Pacific Coast and was one of the first to show paintings of Sierra scenery in the Eastern cities. In time it became apparent that artists were an ever-increasing power in advertising the regions which were newly opened to the public. Recognizing this, the Baltimore and Ohio got some elegant publicity for its "picturesque" route along the Potomac and the Monongahela into West Virginia when, in 1857, the railroad invited twenty artists and photographers

to enjoy the facilities of a special train which was fitted out with a kitchen car, dining saloon with piano, and a car "for photo purposes." To top it all the train would stop wherever the artists wished to make sketches or take photographs.

To a limited degree there had been "public" parks in this country since the beginning of colonization. When Penn laid out the original plan of Philadelphia he assigned for public use a number of squares, the largest of which had measured ten acres. These were to be graced with trees and not to be built over, except perhaps with a few public buildings. Likewise there were "commons" such as those in England in most of the New England settlements. Primarily intended to serve as pastures, they were also used as parade grounds or for recreational purposes. But how little effort was spent to protect such lands from encroachment was evident in Washington, where L'Enfant's grandiose plan providing for an elaborate park system was abandoned very early and only taken up again seriously in 1909 when the original plan was resurrected.

While all these city-bound areas of minor scale cannot be regarded as nuclei for the later park development, the natural burial grounds outside the cities, with their great numbers of visitors who were not mourners, must definitely be regarded as steps in the direction of conservation and the beginning of the park movement. It seems a logical sequence that we should find that William Cullen Bryant was the first to advocate a public park in New York, a park that would be on a scale which up to that time had been unheard of. Although Bryant had discussed the subject privately as early as 1836, his first public plea was published in the *New York Evening Post* on July 3, 1844. While there is no evidence that Bryant was influenced by the scenic cemetery movement, the author of "Thanatopsis," "The Burial," "A Forest Hymn," and "An Indian at the Burial Place of His Father," must have been deeply impressed by the rural cemeteries developing throughout the country. Bryant was joined in his efforts by Andrew Jackson Downing, the landscape architect. In his *Horticulturist* of 1849, Downing asked, "If thirty thousand persons visit a cemetery in a single season, would not a large public garden be especially a matter of curious investigation?". . .

With such eloquent advocates as Bryant and Downing behind it, the proposal for a public park in New York was well accepted, and in 1851 the first act was passed authorizing the acquisition of the necessary lands. The appointment of Frederick Law Olmsted as a superintendent of the project initiated a new era in the best possible way. Olmsted had been a friend and pupil of Downing and had also garnered experience in Europe. After some years of fruitful work in establishing [Central Park], Olmsted . . . gave up his position in May, 1863, and accepted another as superintendent of the mining estates of General Fremont, in Mariposa, [California]. . .

Even after the first excitement over the California Gold Rush had died down, the East learned little about the beauty spots of the newly acquired territory of California. None but the hardiest traveler, and certainly no "tourists," would have been willing to stand the overland trek or either of the wearisome routes by sea. It is significant that one of the first big news stories to come out of California that was not concerned with gold was a show-business stunt. In 1852 the Calaveras Grove of Big Trees was discovered. The next year, two unscrupulous businessmen, George Gale and a companion, stripped one of the Big Trees, the "Mother of the Forest," 315 feet in height and 61 feet in circumference, up to the height of 116 feet, and shipped the bark East for a show in some of the seaboard cities, and then at the Crystal Palace exhibition in Sydenham, London, in 1854. . . . The show turned out to be unsuccessful since, "owing to the immensity of the circumference, nobody would believe that the bark had come from one tree, and finally, being branded as a humbug, the exhibition had to be ended." While this was going on in London, the widely read *Gleason's Pictorial* published a protest by a Californian to whom it seemed a "cruel idea, a perfect desecration to cut down such a splendid tree . . . in Europe such a national production would have been cherished and protected by law; but in this money-making-go-ahead community, thirty or forty thousand dollars are paid for it and the purchaser chops it down and ships it off for a shilling show. We hope that no one will conceive the idea of purchasing Niagara Falls for the same purpose.". . . However trifling the incident may seem to us now, it aroused a great deal of sentiment in the East, and caused people to ponder their duty of protecting nature against the vandalism of enterprising businessmen. At the same time it undoubtedly stimulated great interest in the wonders of California.

The great event in California discoveries, the opening up of the Yosemite [Valley], was publicized with much less fanfare than the Calaveras tree murder. The account in the *Daily Alta California* about the scenic wonders of the valley discovered by the punitive expeditionary force of 1851 against the "Yosemitos" Indians created no stir outside the state. An article published in the *Mariposa Gazette* of July 12, 1855, by James M. Hutchings, whose activities from then on were to be dedicated to the valley, was of broader interest. Real recognition in the East came in 1856, when the *Country Gentleman* republished an article by the *California Christian Advocate* which declared the "Yo-hem-i-ty" valley to be "the most striking natural wonder on the Pacific" and predicted that it would ultimately become a place of great resort. Hutchings started his *California Magazine* in the same year and gave Yosemite good publicity in it. In 1855 and 1856 a California pioneer artist, Thomas A. Ayres, made his first sketches at the valley; some of these were lithographed and spread widely over the East. By 1856 Yosemite had become so well known throughout the nation that T. Richardson who published the first illustrated hand book of American travel of general importance, dedicated about 125 words and one illustration of Mirror Lake to the now celebrated valley of the Yosemite. Here the scenery was called "perhaps the most remarkable in the United States, and perhaps in the world." With such nation-wide publicity the fame of Yosemite was bound to grow year by year.

With so much interest devoted to Yosemite by travelers, journalists, and writers from the East, it would be fascinating to know who in California was taking active interest in the destiny of the valley. . . . The men who were recommended as the first commissioners of the Yosemite grant are most likely those who helped to prepare the act. They were Professor John F. Morse, Israel Ward Raymond, and Frederick Law Olmsted. Of Morse we know only that he was a well-thought-of physician in San Francisco. About Raymond we are better informed. It was he who addressed the decisive letter to Senator John Conness urging him to present a bill concerning Yosemite to Congress. Raymond was the California representative of the Central American Steamship Transit Company of New York. He was known to have been a public-spirited citizen, and certainly did not take this step to further any of his business interests. Altogether, it is quite safe to assume that as a whole the group of men promoting the interests of Yosemite did so for idealistic reasons. This is demonstrated in the measures they recommended and pushed. . . .

Conness was able to introduce the bill on March 28, 1864. There was some discussion on the floor of the Senate in which Conness stated that the bill had come to him from various gentlemen in California "of fortune, of taste and of refinement," that the General Land Office also took great interest in the bill, and that there was "no other condition of things like this one on earth." Finally he referred to the sorry incident of the killing of the Calaveras tree in 1853. The bill was passed, and on June 29, 1864, it was signed by President Lincoln.

So far nothing was extraordinary about the Yosemite grant, and national public opinion certainly was not aroused by the federal action; grants to states were given quite frequently. However, there was something peculiar about this grant, and as it happened, it was destined to set a precedent of real importance. The grant was given "upon the express conditions that the premises shall be held for public use, resort and recreation, shall be held inalienable for all time." These terms implied that no profit was to be expected from the new institution. Probably it was assumed that at least all costs of upkeep would be offset by revenue from leases or privileges; at any rate, Congress took no responsibility. What was really new about the grant was the fact that it served a strictly nonutilitarian purpose.

The year 1868 brought John Muir to

California. His profound devotion to the Sierra initiated a new era in spreading the glory of Yosemite. His enthusiasm is well epitomized in his letter inviting Emerson to Yosemite. "I invite you to join me in a month's worship with Nature in the high temples of the great Sierra Crown beyond our holy Yosemite. It will cost you nothing save the time and very little of that, for you will be mostly in Eternity." In spite of his age, the sixty-seven year old Emerson accepted the invitation and braved the hardships of a journey to Yosemite. In May, 1871, he arrived in the valley. This is what he jotted down in his journal as his first impression: "In Yosemite, grandeur of these mountains perhaps unmatched in the globe; for here they strip themselves like athletes for exhibition and stand perpendicular granite walls, showing their entire height, and wearing a liberty cap of snow on the head."

With Yosemite ranking so high in national favor, the propagators of projects for other scenic areas of some importance were busy trying to get them nationally recognized and protected. There were, of course, many such areas of more or less doubtful value, and their evaluation and recognition took its due course. One of the major areas was that of Niagara Falls. Claims had been made in 1835 that the falls were "the property of civilized mankind." Since 1850 the legislature of New York was lobbied in favor of a bill to protect the falls "against waste and degradation." Once more Olmsted was among those who supported protective legislation. This was finally passed in 1883.

The Yellowstone case had been settled more than a decade earlier by the act of March 1, 1872, which created Yellowstone National Park. . . . [But], the "national park idea" has a very respectable pedigree and was anything but new in 1870.

PETER J. SCHMITT (b. 1936) has plunged into the
relatively unexplored seas of popular culture to write
about the attitude of the average turn-of-the-century
American toward nature. His thesis that nature
appreciation is an *urban* phenomenon deserves careful
attention. Read Schmitt with an eye to comparing the
priorities of his subjects to those discussed in the next
selection by Arthur Ekirch. Does the comparison
suggest the potential for a schism in the nature
movement?

Peter J. Schmitt

Back to Nature

Wild nature has changed almost as
much as an image in American rhetoric as
it has in its physical features. The first
settlers once fought against "barbarism"
to preserve what they knew as culture
and sophistication. But after the Revolution, Americans fashioned a new identity
for themselves. Fortified with European
Romanticism, they took nature and
not civilization as the common demoni-
nator of the new republic. Fourth of July
orators proclaimed that American repub-
licans were products, not victims, of the
wilderness. Thomas Jefferson wrote that
sturdy yeoman farmers shielded from the
artificiality of commerce and city life,
lived lives of quiet simplicity as the
"chosen people of god."

Jefferson's belief developed into a
popular myth: one of those "attitudes"
James M. Williams described as "generally prevalent ways of reacting of which
people become conscious only incidentally as they try to drill them into their
children or as they meet people of contrary attitudes." In 1893, Frederick Jackson Turner worked the agrarian attitude
into "The Significance of the Frontier
in American History." But Turner spoke
to the American Historical Association
at a Columbian Exposition which celebrated America's urban and industrial
future. Americans might still want their
Presidents born on the farm in 1893, but
they hardly expected a working farmer.
Turner accepted Jefferson's dichotomy

between rural good and urban evil, and he noted with a touch of sadness that frontier agriculture and frontier virtue were giving way to urban complexity. Later historians, most notably Richard Hofstadter and Henry Nash Smith, continued to interpret the imagery of factory and farm, of city and country, even of sophistication and simplicity, as clearly antithetical. Smith identified "nature" as a source of moral virtue, with agriculture as a way of life. He argued, however, that "the static ideas of virtue and happiness and peace drawn from the bosom of the virgin wilderness . . . proved quite irrelevant for a society committed to the ideas of civilization and progress." Leo Marx declared in *The Machine in the Garden* that America's continuing enthusiasm for the out-of-doors represented a flight from reality into "naïve and anarchic primitivism." George Mowry called this enthusiasm a vitiating "social nostalgia" which "America's ruling economic classes" stimulated because they found "rural virtues" politically useful. . . .

Americans turning "back to nature". . . responded to a philosophy only faintly related to the pattern of thought which Richard Hofstadter and others have called "agrarianism." Simply put, this urban response valued nature's spiritual impact above its economic importance; it might better be called "Arcadian." Those who looked to nature for a living had categorically settled for something less than Arcadia; the man on the street, not the man on the land, might better benefit from "natural" resources. Webster's *Dictionary* cited John Burroughs in 1899 to demonstrate that "Arcadia" as a word meant little more than a "scene of simple pleasure and untroubled quiet." As a place it lay somewhere on the urban fringe, easily accessible and mildly wild, the goal of a "nature movement" led by

teachers and preachers, bird-watchers, socialites, scout leaders, city-planners, and inarticulate commuters, all of whom applauded William Smythe when he offered in *City Homes on Country Lanes* "the cream of the country and the cream of the city, leaving the skim-milk for those who like that sort of thing.". . .

Men trying to cope with the pressures of urbanization at the turn of the century worked hardest to define the role of nature in an industrial society. Then a whole generation of "literary commuters" took it upon themselves to translate nature into urban terms. . . . From the 1880's on into the 1920's, middle-class journalists tried to combine country life and city culture in essays calculated to appeal to urban readers. . . . Other nature enthusiasts took Arcadia out of books and tried to locate it in life, first for adults and then, more poignantly perhaps, for children. By the middle of the nineteenth century, garden suburbs, city parks, and country estates began to show the influence of landscape designers. . . . Psychologists, sociologists, and educators developed insights into urban behavior that suggested society could not survive without nature. Instinctivists, environmentalists, and crowd psychologists all supposed that man was not made for urban life. . . . Fresh Air Funds and summer camps for city children multiplied rapidly after the 1880's. The Woodcraft Indians, the Sons of Daniel Boone, the Campfire Girls, and the Boy Scouts offered outdoor exposure to city children. At the end of the nineteenth century more and more educators came to feel the schools must provide the contact with nature that city children lacked. Bluebirds and bean-sprouts had a decidedly rural savor, but "nature-study" was not designed for rural schools, and not intended to make farmers of city children.

Enthusiasts claimed the country was in

the midst of a full-scale return to nature. They cited increasing state and national park statistics, the growth of commuter railways, and a variety of other sources to back their contention. Yet it always seemed that Arcadia was easier to find in literature. Twentieth-century readers found a steady stream of nature essays and suburban self-help advice in newspapers and popular magazines. Children in extraordinary numbers enjoyed the outdoor adventures of the Bobbsey Twins and the Rover Boys. Their elders put "nature romances" such as those of Gene Stratton-Porter and Harold Bell Wright on best-seller lists over and over again. . . .

As the twentieth century approached, the "back-to-nature" movement shifted from being a luxury of the rich to a preoccupation of an urban middle-class. Ordinary city dwellers longed for contact with the natural world, and headed for the wilderness and the suburban backyard. Sportsmen tried to capture by temporary immersion in wild nature what wilderness-lover Robert Marshall once called "the ecstasy in non-intellectual adventure." Others combined country life and city convenience as commuters. . . . "It is becoming more and more apparent that the ideal life is that which combines something of the social and intellectual advantages and physical comforts of the city with the inspiration and peaceful joys of the country," Cornell educator Liberty Bailey wrote in 1901. . . .

Middle-class merchants and professional men had begun to look for a place in the country as soon as railroads radiated outward from major cities in the nineteenth century. . . . As early as 1869, the Reverend William Murray described an area the size of Connecticut, a wilderness lying at the gates of New York, in a little volume called *Adventures in the Wilderness or Camp-Life in the Adiron-* *dacks.* "In beauty of scenery, in health-giving qualities, in the easy and romantic manner of its sporting," he wrote, the Adirondacks were a paradise. Murray's book spurred a rush of city sportsmen to such entry ports as Plattsburg and St. Regis. The rustic hotels and accessible scenery of the Adirondacks became a mecca for urban intellectuals. . . .

The rise of the gentleman sportsman and his Arcadian values brought a decline in the prestige of men who hunted for a living. Professional shooters found "market-hunting" a profitable industry at a time when every cookbook insisted that game dinners were part of gracious living. Working from midsummer to late spring, these men made hunting a steady business. "Battery" blinds hidden on feeding grounds and punt guns which fired as much as four pounds of fine shot enabled them to sell their ducks and geese by the barrel. One New York storage plant offered nearly 42,000 game birds for sale in 1902. When New York outlawed the sale of game in 1911, New York City firms reported 190,000 birds in cold storage.

Men who shot for the market and men who shot for the pot were equally disreputable in the sportsman's code. By the twentieth century, in fact, "pot shot" had entered American slang as an act of cowardice and ill-breeding. Elisha Lewis declared the pot hunter "the most disgusting, the most selfish, the most unmanly, the most heartless" of the hunting fraternity. He killed "without regard to etiquette, humanity, law, or even the common decencies of life," and all because he was hungry. To Robert Roosevelt, men who made a business of hunting were no better than "loafing, disreputable, tavern-haunting poachers."

Sportsman and sentimentalist alike proposed legislation to discourage those who "sordidly shoot for the frying pan," as William Hornaday put it. Restrictive legislation was nothing new in the 1880's and '90's. New York first protected quail, ruffed grouse, and turkey in 1708. Deer were protected in Massachusetts from 1718 to 1720, in Virginia in 1772, and in Vermont from 1865 to 1897. North Carolina agreed that property owners had a right to post their lands against hunters in 1784. But such laws were sporadic and in no way restricted the market on which native hunters depended. By 1900, however, the days of market hunting were numbered. In 1896, the Supreme Court declared that wild game belonged to the state and not to the landowner in *Geer v. Connecticut.* Six western states prohibited the sale of game before 1900, and New York's closing of the nation's largest markets in 1911 paved the way for the final ending of market shooting through the Migratory Bird Treaty Act of 1918. Thus wild game moved from a profitable crop to an aesthetic resource, protected for public enjoyment and the sportsman's pleasure. . . .

As early as the 1850's, city sportsmen united in informal associations to ensure the company of social equals. Hunting clubs soon appropriated the better shooting grounds on such famous waters as the Chesapeake Bay and Currituck Sound, offering collectively to members the sport and comfort which none singly could afford. By the end of the century, the hunting club's suburban equivalent, the "country club," developed from the same desire for an appropriately private, rural landscape. . . . As a convenient compromise with wild nature, the country club promised at the turn of the century "to be the safety valve of an overworked nation.". . .

Wild nature seemed increasingly remote to many city dwellers at the turn of the century, but they could surround themselves with its symbols. For those who could afford them there were the lilypads and morning glories of Tiffany art glass and the nature themes woven in oriental carpets. For the less fortunate, the twining vines of *Art Nouveau* graced lampshades and picture frames, paper weights and candle sticks, silverware and bookplates, inkstands and hair brushes. Concert-goers listened to Edward McDowell's *Woodland Sketches* and *New England Idylls,* the latter composed in McDowell's log-cabin studio near Peterboro, New Hampshire. "To a Wild Rose" and "By a Meadow Brook," like the "Joy of Autumn," "In Deep Woods" and "From a Log Cabin," seemed perfectly programmed for urban audiences. Innumerable artists tried to capture nature in murky pastels or the kind of poetry climaxed by that triumph of sentiment over style, Joyce Kilmer's "Trees." For those who hesitated to "rough it" out-of-doors, there were balsam pillows embroidered with scenes of far-off wilderness and "pillow-tents" that offered outdoor air with indoor comfort. California bungalow designers even included a thoroughly Arcadian "sleeping porch," a sign of status which George F. Babbitt proudly claimed. . . .

At whatever level it appeared, from nature-study classroom to the White House, the Arcadian myth embodied an urban response to nature that seemed most appropriate for an urban age. No matter how indifferently it actually transformed city life, most Americans came to link it with status and sophistication. Many adopted the role with no understanding of its intricate philosophy. Yet in so far as they believed that country life and city culture offered more in conjunction than as opposites, they seemed to welcome the contact with "Nature."

In the Progressive era of the early twentieth century the American conservation movement enjoyed its first significant taste of public favor. In reading this essay by ARTHUR A. EKIRCH, JR. (b. 1915) ask yourself why Americans between 1900 and 1910 were ready to be aroused by the conservationists. What were the diverse sources of Progressive conservation's appeal? For a more critical assessment of conservation in the era of Theodore Roosevelt and Gifford Pinchot turn to Grant McConnell's analysis in the next reading.

Arthur A. Ekirch, Jr.

The Utilitarian Emphasis

Conservation did not become an important American ideology until the 1900's. Only then was it represented by an increasing body of systematic ideas and ardent corps of dedicated disciples. Although there were other influential spokesmen, Theodore Roosevelt and Gifford Pinchot probably did the most to make conservation a popular crusading idea, though, of course, it still meant many different things to various individuals. Moreover, in some of its aspects, it was not new but was as old as American civilization.

During the nineteenth century there had been no lack of a romantic interest in nature, nor of enthusiastic exploration of the American landscape by writers, artists, and travelers. [Henry David] Thoreau and the transcendentalists made nature the center of a philosophy of harmony and balance, and an occasional pioneer like [George Perkins] Marsh called attention to the need for conserving natural resources. But America was too much a land of plenty to be worried over alleged or impending scarcities. Instead of diminishing with the nineteenth century, this confident attitude seemed to increase with the settlement of the trans-Mississippi West after the Civil War. Only the so-called closing of the frontier—at least in the sense of free and easy exploitation of the West—made conservation the serious concern of some Americans.

From Arthur A. Ekirch, Jr., *Man and Nature in America* (New York, Columbia University Press, 1963), pp. 81–92, 94–100. Footnotes omitted.

Nevertheless, for many people, and especially for Westerners, conservation continued to arouse suspicion and hostility. They associated it with the idea of the saving or nonuse of natural resources. Since the prosperity of the West depended on the development of its forests and mineral wealth, Westerners were apt to dismiss conservation as an artificial concept tinged with Eastern romantic and humanitarian notions. Although most conservationist leaders denied that they intended anything more than the curbing of waste and the carefully planned use of natural resources, this view was to some extent a later defense rather than an original argument. Certainly a prominent goal of the conservation movement was the preservation of natural beauty spots and wild life reserves as national parks. And the movement also stressed the necessity of saving forests and mineral resources for the use of future generations. Conservationists were sometimes accused therefore of being nature lovers or socialist planners. But whatever the inner rationale or philosophy of the movement, conservation did seem to point toward the goal of man living in better balance or harmony with his natural environment.

Appreciation of the new wonders of nature as revealed in the Far West played an important part in gaining more general American support for conservation. Along with gold seekers and homesteaders, California in the 1850's was host to a smaller number of visitors who came to admire the gigantic beauty of the Mariposa forest in the Yosemite Valley. After the Civil War the railroads provided easier, swifter access to the West, and the Rockies, Yosemite, Yellowstone, and the Grand Canyon all attracted increasing attention on the part of American literary men and artists. Horace Greeley visited Yosemite in 1859, and after the war [Ralph Waldo] Emerson, while in California, received John Muir's enthusiastic invitation to "join me in a month's worship with Nature in the high temples of the great Sierra Crown beyond our holy Yosemite. It will cost you nothing save the time and very little of that for you will be mostly in Eternity." Henry Adams went along on Clarence King's geological exploration of the Fortieth Parallel, and in 1872 William Cullen Bryant edited a two-volume work entitled *Picturesque America,* with illustrations by some of the best American artists. Albert Bierstadt was already famous for his paintings of Far Western scenes, and now in the West for the first time photography began to provide competition for the landscape artist.

Although John Burroughs, Muir's fellow naturalist, had some difficulty in understanding the latter's enthusiastic devotion to the California country, others found in the rugged primeval scenery of the Far West the same kind of a harmony of man with nature that was Burroughs' own main interest. In view of the speed with which the United States had spanned the continent, there was an understandable anxiety to preserve at least some parts of the West from the all-conquering march of civilization. The unique wonders of such sites as Yosemite, Yellowstone, and the Grand Canyon were being portrayed for Easterners by a number of important writers and artists, and in 1872 Congress established Yellowstone as the country's first national park. Other scenic sites were also preserved as national parks, but the program developed slowly until the First World War. There was considerable opposition in Congress to the notion that the government was going into the business of recreation and amusement. At the same time many of the park areas remained inaccessible, and Western tourist travel was confined largely to the Yosemite Valley and Yellowstone National Park. Nevertheless, by 1916, when the National Park Service was created, it had some 37 national parks and monuments placed under its administrative direction.

Although not established as a national monument until 1908, and as a national park until 1919, the Grand Canyon of the Colorado was perhaps the most awesome of the natural wonders of the American Far West. It also became probably the most widely celebrated after the dramatic journey down the gorge led by Major John Wesley Powell in 1869. . . .

In the 1870's Powell continued his exploration of the West, but by 1874 he reported: "There is now left within the territory of the United States no great unexplored region, and exploring expeditions are no longer needed for general purposes." Instead, "It is of the most immediate and pressing importance that a general survey should be made for the purpose of determining the special areas which can . . . be redeemed by irrigation." Four years later he published his noteworthy *Report on the Lands of the Arid Region of the United States*. Observing that two fifths of the United States was arid territory, Powell sketched out the needs of the West for conservation and irrigation. In 1879 Congress appropriated funds for the creation of the United States Geological Survey as an over-all agency to direct the work of the states and Federal agencies in connection with the conservation and protection of the national domain. Powell as director of the survey concerned himself mostly with water-power sites, irrigation projects, and mineral resources. He was a foe of the private water companies which, he believed, wanted to achieve irrigation for farm land without proper conservation practices.

Opposed to Social Darwinian notions of an automatic progress by discovering and obeying the laws of nature, Powell declared in an address in 1883 on the Methods of Evolution: "When a man loses faith in himself, and worships nature, and subjects himself to the government of the laws of physical nature, he lapses into stagnation, where mental and moral miasma is bred. All that makes man superior to the beast is the result of his own endeavor to secure happiness. . . . Man lives in the desert by guiding a river thereon and fertilizing the sands with its waters, and the desert is covered with fields and gardens and homes."

Powell's disbelief in an automatic evolutionary progress and his faith in government action and regulation were at variance with the prevailing American mood, but they pointed in the direction which most leaders of the conservation movement followed. Powell's nationalism was moulded by his Civil War army experience and a career as a government scientist. Other leading conservationists were also men of strong nationalistic feelings, and many were familiar with European practice in the regulation of forest preserves and other natural resources. The experience of both Europe and America indicated that the forests which had once covered most of the northern temperate zone were in large part already destroyed. George Perkins Marsh, for example, feared that the forests of the United States would be ravaged in the same fashion as those in Europe. "It is certain," he wrote, "that a desolation, like that which has overwhelmed many once beautiful and fertile regions of Europe, awaits an important part of the territory of the United States . . . unless prompt measures are taken to check the action of destructive causes already in operation."

The preservation of timber resources,

which seemed the most pressing conservation problem after the Civil War, also attracted the greatest public attention and sympathy, although the Federal government did not become concerned with forest conservation until late in the nineteenth century. Earlier fears over the possibility of a shortage of ship-construction timber died out with the shift to iron and steel in naval vessels. But by the last third of the century appeals were being made for public action to conserve forest resources. A tree-planting campaign resulted in the national celebration of Arbor Day, and in 1873 Congress passed the Timber Culture Act, making the growing of a certain number of trees a consideration for receiving a quarter section of the public domain. The American Association for the Advancement of Science urged Congress to investigate the condition of the nation's forests, and, in 1875, $2,000 was appropriated to permit the Department of Agriculture to undertake a study of forest conditions in the United States. At this time Secretary of the Interior Carl Schurz . . . launched a campaign to stop timber removal from the public domain. In 1877 he recommended that all Federal timber lands be withdrawn from entry under the pre-emption and homestead laws. Although Schurz's efforts met with no immediate success, in the 1880's some of the individual states began to take action in regard to their own forest lands, and public interest continued to grow.

The campaign for forest conservation was given specialized sponsorship in 1882 when the American Forestry Congress was organized. A prominent figure at the Congress was Bernhard E. Fernow, who later became the first professional forester employed by the Federal government. Fernow had been trained at the Forest Academy of Munden in Prussia, and he discussed the development of forest care in Germany, pointing out that reforestation extended back in time as far as Charlemagne. The Forestry Congress also received a special communication from the Royal Chief Forester of the German Empire. The knowledge of Europe's experience encouraged American conservationists to seek similar government regulations and controls in the United States. But, at the same time, it was this aspect of the conservation movement that conflicted most with traditional American beliefs in the free exploitation of the national domain. Westerner's fears of Federal control seemed substantiated when in 1889 the American Forestry Association, successor to the Congress, and the American Association for the Advancement of Science urged Congress to set up forest reserves and temporarily withdraw all forest lands from sale. Finally, on March 2, 1891, in the Act to Repeal the Timber Culture Laws, Congress authorized the President to establish forest reserves from the lands in the public domain. Both Presidents Harrison and Cleveland took the needed action, but Clevand in 1893 refused to withdraw more forest land until adequate provision was made for the care of the existing government reserves. This situation was partly corrected by the Act of June 4, 1897, providing that "No public forest reservation shall be established, except to improve and protect the forests within the reservation, or for the purposes of securing favorable conditions of water flows, and to furnish a continuous supply of timber for the use and necessities of the citizens of the United States."

By the turn of the century conservationists could be divided into two groups: those who favored a planned and scientific use of natural resources; and lovers of nature who wished to preserve the natural landscape unspoiled, as nearly as possible, by civilization. For example, nature lovers and big-game hunters wanted the national forests kept inviolate as parks or game preserves, while stockmen and lumber companies favored the use of these lands for grazing and commercial timber. Both groups of conservationists had already achieved some success in their attempts to influence government policy. Wildlife preserves and national parks helped keep nature in its pristine state. And, at the same time, conservation was becoming closely tied to the progressives' urgings of an efficient use of natural resources under government controls. Progressives and conservationists criticized the traditional American emphasis on competition as leading to overproduction and consumption, with resultant waste and inefficiency. Such practices were linked to monopoly, but monopolists were also being prosecuted for limiting production, although in this they would seem to have been supporting conservation. As one authority, in commenting on Theodore Roosevelt's inconsistent efforts, observed: "The trust-buster and conservationist are strange bedfellows."

Although some students of the conservation movement have argued that the "organized conservationists were concerned more with economic justice and democracy in the handling of resources than with mere prevention of waste," it is perhaps more correct to say that the conservationists advocated the kind of efficiency and scientific management which they believed could be best achieved through government regulation and control. Frequently hostile to laissez faire and traditional American individualism, conservationists accepted Theodore Roosevelt's concept of a regulated monopoly, and the conservationist gospel of efficiency became a part of both big government and big business. "The conserva-

tion movement," one of its recent students has declared, "did not involve a reaction against large-scale corporate business, but, in fact, shared its views in a mutual revulsion against unrestrained competition and undirected economic development. Both groups placed a premium on large-scale capital organization, technology, and industry-wide cooperation and planning to abolish the uncertainties and waste of competitive resource use."

Considered in the above terms, conservation was an exercise in public and business administration, rather than an example of democracy at work. It was not a case of the people versus selfish interests. Frequently big business favored conservation, while small grass-roots farmers and entrepreneurs distrusted the degree of centralized control it involved. Finally, conservation became a matter of patriotism and of national security in the midst of growing imperialistic world rivalries. The great exponent of this side of conservation was Gifford Pinchot, who declared that "the conservation of natural resources is the basis, and the only permanent basis, of national success. . . . The planned and orderly development and conservation of our natural resources is the first duty of the United States."

Gifford Pinchot, who has been called America's First Forester, was born a Connecticut Yankee on August 11, 1865. His parents were wealthy and on the father's side descended from French Huguenots who had settled in Milford, Pennsylvania. After studying botany at Yale, Gifford, who had determined at his father's suggestion upon a career in forestry, traveled in Europe where he could observe at first hand the latest scientific and practical methods in forest care. On his return to the United States, he inspected some of the timber lands of the Phelps Dodge Company, and then he became forester in charge of George W. Vanderbilt's Biltmore estate in North Carolina. On the Vanderbilt lands, he was given the task and opportunity "to prove what America did not yet understand, that trees could be cut and the forest preserved at one and the same time." His success at Biltmore and in other consulting positions led to an appointment in 1896 to the National Forest Commission. This gave Pinchot a foothold within the formal conservation movement and valuable contacts in the Federal government, so that on May 11, 1898, he was named head of the Forestry Division of the Department of Agriculture.

In his new position Pinchot had to move carefully at first. Since forest reserves were under the jurisdiction of the General Lands Office of the Department of the Interior, he was literally a forester without forests. Finally, in 1905, after a long struggle in Congress in which he was aided by President Roosevelt, all forest reserves were placed under the jurisdiction of the Department of Agriculture and Pinchot's Bureau of Forests. In the meantime Pinchot had begun a campaign of education to persuade private owners that their timber lands could be scientifically cut to yield a continuing profit without destroying the forests. . . .

A great help to Pinchot, and a tremendous encouragement to the cause of conservation in general, was Theodore Roosevelt's entrance into the White House. Unsparing in his criticism of the so-called nature fakers, the President was keenly interested in the preservation of the natural beauty as well as the rich resources of the country. On his first presidential visit to the Far West in 1903, he toured North Dakota and the Yellowstone, accompanied by John Burroughs. In California, he and John Muir spent a weekend in the forests of the Yosemite, where the naturalist had a good chance to talk freely with the President concerning his ideas on conservation. Although Theodore Roosevelt lent a sympathetic ear to the nature lovers like Muir and Burroughs—setting aside the Grand Canyon as a national monument in 1908, for example—his major contribution to the conservation movement was the practical political support that he gave in Washington to leaders of the cause like Pinchot. The latter, in turn, although he deprecated the sentimentalism of those like Muir, was considerably aided in securing popular backing for conservation by the activities of the nature organizations, civic improvement groups, and garden clubs that were springing up across the nation.

Like Roosevelt, but in advance of most public officials of his day, Pinchot saw clearly the close relationship between propaganda, control of public opinion, political lobbies, lawmaking, and appropriations. To mobilize public opinion behind the cause of conservation, he used the Bureau of Forests to conduct an extensive publicity service. The Bureau provided technical information, lantern slides, and other materials for schools and associations, and for lecturers, teachers, and writers, while Pinchot and his subordinates themselves did much writing and speaking and issued frequent news releases. In a letter in 1903 Pinchot pointed to the value of good public relations. "Nothing permanent," he said, "can be accomplished in this country unless it is backed by a sound public sentiment. The greater part of our work, therefore, has consisted in arousing a general interest in practical forestry throughout the country and in gradually changing public sentiment toward a more conservative treatment of forest lands.". . .

Conservation, of course, included more

than scientific forestry practices. The preservation of water and mineral resources was also a matter of growing concern in the 1900's. Under Theodore Roosevelt the government began to withdraw coal lands still within the public domain from public sale. Of still greater interest to the West were water resources — both for irrigation and power. To cope with the problem of the vast arid areas of the Western United States, which had attracted the attention of Major Powell in the 1870's, Congress at first confined itself to donating land for irrigation purposes. The next step came with the Newlands Act of 1902, creating the Reclamation Service in charge of Frederick H. Newell, a government conservationist second only to Pinchot in his influence on the President. The Newlands or Reclamation Act assigned the receipts of land sales in the arid states to the construction of storage reservoirs or other permanent irrigation works. The Federal government by thus providing the land and water for irrigated farming encouraged anew the possibility of homesteading. In addition, the forestry program helped to build natural watersheds to conserve runoff waters and to prevent excessive erosion of the soil.

Finally, to establish some over-all plan in regard to the water resources of the nation, President Roosevelt created the Inland Waterways Commission. Stating that his action was "influenced by broad considerations of national policy," the President pointed out that the time had come to merge "local projects and uses of inland waters in a comprehensive plan designed for the benefit of the entire country." As Roosevelt implied, the Commission was really intended as the beginning of an integrated conservation policy. Further indication of this broad national purpose for the Commission was

the prominent part in its work assumed by the conservationist leaders Pinchot and W. J. McGee. Although the President credited Pinchot with the idea for the Commission, the latter indicated that it was McGee who was the real author. McGee, whom Pinchot called "the scientific brains" of the conservation movement, also provided it with a rationale or plan of action. He had served with Powell in the Geological Survey and, like Powell and Pinchot, was a strong advocate of positive government action. He believed that conservation should be considered as a whole comprehensive movement and not be limited to any single natural resource.

To further a broad conservation policy and carry forward the idea behind the Inland Waterways Commission, Pinchot urged President Roosevelt to call all the state governors together in a national conservation conference. Roosevelt heartily approved this suggestion, and in the final year of his second administration the early conservation movement also reached its climax in the famous Conference of Governors at the White House in May, 1908. By this time, as Pinchot later recalled, conservation had come to have the connotations and unity later ascribed to the movement. It emphasized the comprehensive and well-planned management of all natural resources according to sound ethical and economic standards.

Pinchot's utilitarian definition embraced the practical governmental aspects of conservation to which the agenda of the Conference of Governors was confined. With the help of McGee and Commissioner Newell, he dominated the planning for the Conference and served as its chairman. When Congress withheld an appropriation, Pinchot, according to Gilson Gardner, a reporter friendly to the progressives, paid the Conference expenses and with his mother entertained one thousand guests at a reception in the Washington family mansion.

The two major themes of the Conference were the impending depletion of natural resources and the necessity of their conservation as a matter of national patriotism. In the words of the President to the governors and their advisors and guests: "I have asked you to come together now because the enormous consumption of these resources, and the threat of imminent exhaustion of some of them, due to reckless and wasteful use, once more calls for common effort, common action." McGee, who likened the Conference to a Second Declaration of Independence, had prepared invitations for officers of a number of patriotic societies having nothing to do with conservation. Although the President, believing such invitations inappropriate, personally destroyed them, he nevertheless called conservation fundamentally a question of morality and patriotism. The American people, he feared, did not understand conservation as a "problem of national efficiency, the patriotic duty of insuring the safety and continuance of the Nation.". . .

The Conference of Governors led to the establishment of a National Conservation Commission as a coordinating and fact-finding body. Also, in December, 1908, a Joint Conservation Conference was held between selected state and Federal officials. By this time conservation had become a well-organized movement. The older groups of naturalists with their nature societies and clubs were overshadowed by the new practical, political conservationists led by Pinchot and his fellow government officials. It was not accidental that many of these men were lawyers. After 1909 the rallying

point for the conservationists was the National Conservation Association, which included a number of leading progressives in its membership and which became an effective lobbying body in Washington.

Conservation now involved sizable political and business interests which ignored the older concept of conservation as a balance of nature. Conflicts like the famous Ballinger-Pinchot dispute brought competing interests over the use of resources into the open. But, even more significant was the way in which both government and business were coming to accept conservation in terms of scientific efficiency. Conservation to insure profits and national security was the new progressive goal. In the words of Pinchot's *Fight for Conservation*, "The central thing for which Conservation stands is to make this country the best possible place to live in, both for us and for our descendants. It stands against the waste of the natural resources which cannot be renewed, such as coal and iron: it stands for the perpetuation of the resources which can be renewed, such as food-producing soils and the forests; and most of all it stands for an equal opportunity for every American citizen to get his fair share of benefit from these resources, both now and hereafter." To this Pinchot added: "Conservation stands for the same kind of practical commonsense management of this country by the people that every business man stands for in handling of his own business."

The early conservation movement which came to fruition in 1908 was a highly successful, practical propaganda effort intermixed with considerable idealism. It was able to persuade the American public that the natural resources of the West should belong to the nation and to the people as a whole, rather than to the states or to individuals and corporations.

Conservation was thus in logical accord with the Roosevelt era, providing a good example of progressivism at work. As later difficulties testified, it also was part of the problem of reconciling an efficient bureaucracy and strong central government with individual and local interests. Finally, and perhaps most important, it illustrated the President's nationalistic approach and his concern with national security. . . .

Conservation, as defined by Pinchot and his colleagues, had come to mean, not the effort to achieve a balance with nature, but the more efficient planned use of nature's resources. Interpreted in this way, it seemed to provide a popular scientific answer to the new national problems of the twentieth century. It appealed, not only to the progressive reformers' nationalism and patriotism, but also to their interest in social control and planning. It was democratic in a nationalistic rather than individualistic sense. . . . Conservationist ideology was one of the component parts of the idea of a planned society. As the old hope of achieving a natural automatic balance and harmony faded, new visions of reaching the same goal via conscious scientific planning emerged more brightly. The Utopian dreams of agrarian reformers and romantic transcendentalists seemed to hold less and less reality in the industrialized mechanized world of the twentieth century. But the old ideal of a proper balance between the forces of man and nature might nevertheless be attained through purposeful planning and effort. The conservation movement was a first step in this direction, providing a common ground for the growing faith in science and government regulation that characterized so much of the Progressive era. This degree of scientific planning and centralized control involved in conservation was often overlooked in the excitement of the nationalism and patriotism invoked by Roosevelt and Pinchot to gain popular backing for their cause. But the conservation movement was one of the bridges from the individualism of the nineteenth century to the collectivism of the twentieth.

A political scientist, GRANT McCONNELL (b. 1915) is especially interested in the politics of environmental concern. But his essay goes beyond this into the internal tensions of the conservation movement and the reasons for both its successes and its failures. Look for contradictions among the priorities McConnell's subjects espoused. What do you think of the thesis that the Progressive conservationists were only more efficient pioneers, that their perspective in the last analysis was the same as that of frontiersmen? Notice how McConnell explains the recent rise to national prominence and power of organized conservation. What are the major differences between the movement in the Progressive period, in the 1950s, and today?

Grant McConnell

The Failures and Successes of Organized Conservation

Recently one of the scholarly journals carried the observation that the conservation movement "has come of age." In its implicit recognition of the growing effectiveness of conservation, this is a statement in which all of us must take much interest. This paper glances back over some of the history of conservation and looks at some of the reasons why it is possible to say that conservation has come of age.

In 1954, which is really not so very long ago, I made an assessment of the conservation movement, being curious about the meaning of conservation and what it amounted to as a political movement. Here is a bit of what I wrote then. . . :

"Today we see a conservation movement that is both different in content and weaker than that which was for a time the most conspicuous political movement alive." In my own defense I hasten to say that the 1954 article was justified on the evidence before us at that time; I think it was correct. But in less than a decade and a half the situation is completely changed.

What has been the nature of the conservation movement in recent years, and in what ways has it changed? Consider what the situation was in 1954. The drive for the Upper Colorado Storage Project was in high gear, and the fate of Dinosaur National Monument and with it the

From Grant McConnell, "Environment and the Quality of Political Life," in Richard Cooley and Geoffrey Wandesforde-Smith, eds., *Congress and the Environment* (Seattle: University of Washington Press, 1970), pp. 3–15. Footnotes omitted.

sanctity of the entire National Park System was all but sealed. Conservation representatives were valiantly testifying before hostile senators from Utah and other Rocky Mountain states. Senator [Arthur] Watkins [Utah], for example, attempted with all the advantages of his official position to break the dignity and courage of David Brower, who was dramatically demonstrating the technical possibility of an alternative plan that would leave Echo Park untouched. One of the facts that Senator Watkins extracted was that the Sierra Club was an organization of a mere eight thousand members. In the Northwest, the Olympic Park had just been subjected to another of its periodic attacks. And in the Northwest, also just a year later, it became apparent that the North Cascades were marked for the sort of "intensive management" by the Forest Service that could only spell destruction of their unique values of wilderness and beauty. A handful of people met in a living room in Auburn, Washington, to discuss the problem; it was a very glum occasion.

Contrast this situation with that of the first decade of this century. The conservation movement was apparently the strongest political force in the country. It was led by an unusually gifted politician, Gifford Pinchot, a man who not only had a very firm idea of what he was about but also had the ear of a very sympathetic President. He was largely responsible for the act establishing the Forest Service and for creating the administrative doctrine by which the agency has been run since. In 1908 he and his chief held a conference of the governors of the United States, justices of the Supreme Court, members of Congress and representatives of some sixty-eight national societies, and other distinguished individuals. The subject was conservation—conservation of forests, minerals, soils, and water. There was a spate of similar conferences around the country, and "conservation" must have been a word of greater currency then than any other of its length in the English language. And it was in 1908* that the term, "conservation movement," was invented —once again the work of Pinchot and his associates.

On comparing these two times—take the dates of 1908 and 1954—it would seem that after a remarkable beginning there had been a grievous decline and failure. We might even leap to the conclusion that in 1954 there were only shattered remnants left of a one-time crusade. It is true that the term "conservation movement" dates from 1908. It is also true that there was an enormous lot of talk about conservation in the early years of the century. It is also true that in 1954 conservation groups were fighting a steep uphill battle. But there the list stops. Conservation as a cause much antedates the efforts of Pinchot, important as these were. The prodigality and heedless destructiveness of Americans with their natural environment aroused thoughtful men long before the beginning of this century. Perhaps we should begin with Jefferson, who had a keen sensitivity to the soil and the need for its protection. But probably a more reasonable point of beginnings is the publication of a still-great book, *Man and Nature*, by George Perkins Marsh, in 1864. This was a work of science, but it was also something much more, an appeal for morality. Let me quote one passage:

Man has too long forgotten that the earth was given to him for usufruct alone, not for consumption, still less for profligate waste.

---

*The date was 1907 according to Pinchot's autobiography *Breaking New Ground*.—Ed.

Nature has provided against the absolute destruction of any of the elementary material of her works, the thunderbolt and the tornado, the most convulsive throes of even the volcano and earthquake being only the phenomena of decomposition and recomposition. But she has left it within the power of man irreparably to derange the combinations of inorganic matter and of organic life, which through the night of aeons she had been proportioning and balancing, to prepare the earth for his habitation, when in the fullness of time, his Creator should call him forth to enter into its possession.

During the second half of the nineteenth century there was a succession of men of science who turned their efforts to the problem of protecting the natural environment against the dangers which were menacing it. Much as we are inclined to think of American science as influential only in the last few decades, one of its times of glory was the latter part of the nineteenth century. There was the achievement of men such as John Wesley Powell, who personally traced the course of the Colorado River and profoundly affected the development of the U.S. Geological Survey. There were the warning memorials passed by the American Association for the Advancement of Science in 1873 and 1890, which culminated in the establishment of a bureau of forestry in the Department of Agriculture. There was the push given the idea of national forests by the National Academy of Sciences in 1897. And there were other groups and other individuals who got their messages to the ears of the mighty, and together achieved a series of significant checks upon the destructiveness of Americans on their land. Gifford Pinchot, whose own personal passion was the science of forestry, stood in a culminating point of a long line of American scientists. He was less a scientist than some of his predecessors, but he had much greater talent as a politician than any of them, and this was the essential talent. He gained the nearly unqualified support of a strong President at a moment when much hung in the balance.

There are several features which deserve particular attention in this early period. The first is that conservation was hardly a popular movement. The achievements were made by the fortunate influence of a handful of thoughtful men upon a few receptive presidents. The setting aside of the national forests in the first place was anything but the response of government to a great national outcry. On several occasions, in fact, the way land was thus set aside was almost conspiratorial. In substance, the early conservation achievements were the work of an elite—of a few peculiarly well-placed and influential individuals and small groups. In time, of course, the wisdom of these elites has been vindicated by great popular support, but it is clear that this support came considerably later, and it came because the case that the scientists had made was a good one and because they stood firmly on principle. Perhaps it cannot be claimed that true morality always wins, but without the moral stance exemplified by that passage from George Perkins Marsh, what was won would not have endured to become the object of a popular cause.

In the years between 1905 and 1910, Gifford Pinchot put forth mighty efforts to make conservation a popular cause. Not only did he invent a name, coin slogans, and hold meetings—he wrote and spoke endlessly. To him we can be grateful for the fact that nobody today will admit he opposes conservation—to do that would be equivalent to spitting on the flag or decrying motherhood. It is a great advantage. But we should not lose sight of the fact that in hard political terms, he got his real results by virtue of his close personal association with Theodore Roosevelt. When Roosevelt left office and took off for his African safari, the influence of Pinchot quickly faded, and, with it, that of the conservation movement he had invented.

The national forests were firmly established, however, and the gain was solid. But the job of going beyond, to gain for the American people protection of some of those values of which Marsh had spoken during the Civil War, the path of achievement had to continue to be what it had been before—dedicated effort by a small handful of gifted individuals and a few small groups influencing the mighty, trusting always that in time popular support would follow to make achievement secure and lasting. This, in general, is what has happened with the development of the National Park System. With the work of John Muir and a quite small group of his followers, many critical areas of the nation's most magnificent scenery have been set aside. At each moment it has largely been true that few Americans were aware of their stake. But, within a short time after the establishment of each park, the general support has appeared, and we can say that America has, to this date, a good record of preserving its parks.

One other feature of the first part of the century calls for special note. The effort to make conservation a popular movement at that time involved a very particular political philosophy. This was the doctrine of Progressivism. This was undoubtedly inevitable, since conservation was dependent on a particular group of national leaders who were committed to that doctrine. It was not a very sophisticated doctrine, indeed to call it a political philosophy is to dignify it unduly. It is worth noting briefly several of the tenets of Progressivism. In the first place, Progressivism dwelt particularly, in Pinchot's words, on "the greatest good of the greatest number in the long run." That this slogan was a very slightly amended bit of plagiarism seems never to have been appreciated by Pinchot. He was not an intellectually sophisticated man, and all the evidence indicates that he thought he had invented a scientific formula that would lead inevitably to certain and unquestionable results. The fact, of course, was that this formula, minus the bit about the long run, was the invention of an eighteenth-century English philosopher, Jeremy Bentham, and that it was ridden with ambiguity. Specifically, what *kind* of good, and for which people? Are all "goods" equal in nature? And are all desires to be placed on the same plane? Such questions never entered into Pinchot's reflections, at least insofar as we are able to determine from his autobiography, his speeches, or his teachings to his agency. He was a supremely self-assured individual.

These abstract questions would be unimportant were he a mere political philosopher. But, on the contrary, he was a powerful agency head, with something like an eighth of the surface of the United States under his command and with the formation of a whole doctrine under his pen. What this all meant in practice was that the question about the *kind* of good was answered—all goods were equal. It was simply a matter of adding them up. Ultimately, it meant that those which could be measured were to be regarded as the only values that were hard and real. It is not surprising in the American context of the highly materialistic period of the early twentieth century that the dollar proved to be the best unit of measurement. And, at a later date, it has not been surprising to find that a sort of head count (as in the number of people using a bit of wilderness) should be a major test by Pinchot's agency as to whether it was justified in setting aside the area to be unimpaired. Both tests flew in the face of the experience and history that has just been traced. The dollar test was hopelessly biased in favor of material returns—sawlogs, jobs, and so on. The head count test necessarily produced the result that wilderness was less satisfying of the greatest good than a network of logging roads paid for by the logs taken out but providing an abundance of picnic tables in however devastated a landscape. If there is any doubt about this outcome from his outlook—after all, Pinchot was a logical man—consider this authoritative statement: "The object of our forest policy is not to preserve the forests because they are beautiful . . . or because they are refuges for the wild creatures of the wilderness . . . but . . . the making of prosperous homes. . . . Every other consideration becomes secondary." He was an out-and-out materialist, and, not surprisingly, his child, the United States Forest Service, has had great difficulty in surmounting the limitations which he set for it.

This test of the greatest good, moreover, implied something else which has had great importance in the shaping of American public policy. It implied some quasi-mathematical criterion and a kind of scientism in the process of decision making. Professor Samuel P. Hays has characterized conservation in the period of Pinchot and in the tradition that followed him as "the gospel of efficiency." Standing in the tradition briefly outlined above, Pinchot's doctrine implied that when it came down to choices as to which values should be preferred in the use of National Forest land, experts should have

the say and the decision. In choosing, for example, between logging and wilderness, the Forest Service should be allowed to make the determination in the light of its peculiar expertise. This might be well and good if the decisions were merely whether logs could be economically taken out at a given moment, but there is no scientific expertise that can say whether logs are better than wilderness at *any* time. The claim to the power to decide was a claim to an extreme of discretion. This claim was all the more serious for being made in the presence of a materialistic bias of which Pinchot and his followers were unquestioning, and, perhaps, unaware. This characteristic of scientism, at any rate, underlines the degree to which the "conservation movement" started by Pinchot in the early part of the century was less than a popular movement. In a quite ultimate sense it was nondemocratic, although it had pretensions as a democratic movement. But this was democratic in the sense that experts would determine what was the greatest good. Whether by the test of popular support or by that of philosophic intent, conservation in the early period of this century was not a democratic movement.

What we see today, what goes by the old tag of conservation movement, is a different kind of animal. We now behold a movement with a strong popular base. It is not the sort of thing that progressivism fostered, a gathering up of material demands upon the natural resources of the environment, with all demands having equal standing except as they were made by more or fewer people as measured by an elite of experts. We have, rather, a body of belief firmly grounded on a set of principles cherished by a substantial and growing segment of the public. This is a fact of the first political magnitude, one that requires explanation.

In 1954 this was not evident. That period looked, at the time, like one of decline from the period just after the turn of the century. From today's prospect, however, it was a critical moment in a new development. Senator Watkins did not win that argument with David Brower, and Echo Park has not been buried in mud. That little group of eight thousand in the Sierra Club has grown to over seventy thousand. The dismal little group in Auburn worrying about the North Cascades has become the North Cascades Conservation Council, which led the fight for a park in the Cascades through to success. A park has been created in the redwoods. A Wild Rivers System and a National Trail System have been established. All this certainly does not mean that there is now a mighty conservation movement rolling on to inevitable victory everywhere. We cannot forget that the Upper Colorado Project destroyed the grandeur of Glen Canyon and that politicians have deleted significant parts of the North Cascades from the Park Act or that the Redwoods Park is small. What is significant is that today there is a conservation *movement* and that it is grounded firmly in *both* popular support and in principle. It is no longer a matter of a handful of scientists and other enlightened individuals quietly influencing key statesmen to slip actions through which will have genuine public support only at a later time. This is the sense in which it is appropriate to agree that conservation "has come of age."

What accounts for this development? A full explanation would be complex. On the face of things it might seem that the values of great numbers of Americans have changed over the years. In the sense that values are really testable only by choices actually given effect, this is plainly true. But this is to say very little.

There is a genuine possibility that recent generations have wanted different things than their predecessors, but in view of the possibility that the political system may have had a bias in validating some preferences instead of others, casting aspersions on our ancestors as a wholly materialist lot is not justified. If current Americans show more signs of caring for the nonmaterial aspects of their environment, it may well be because the political order has evolved sufficiently to allow such concern to have occasional effect.

There are good grounds for believing that this is the case. Very briefly, the United States is much more of a nation than it has been in the past. It is knit together with roads, airlines, telephones, television, and magazines to a degree difficult to foresee even a relatively few decades ago. The horizons of the average American have vastly expanded so that the inhabitants of Sauk Center and all its real counterparts now share a national culture as never before. Inevitably, this has been reflected in the workings of the political system. Many decisions that were formerly within the exclusive provinces of states and localities are now made in larger arenas, arenas in which an inevitably greater diversity of citizens participate.

Formerly, choices on the allocation of values, as for example between natural beauty and resource exploitation, was largely in the hands of localities and, in fact, was regarded as mainly a private matter. Insofar as the choice lay in the hands of a lumber or a mining company, the choice for exploitation was preordained. But the situation was more complex than this suggests. If the choice were in the hands—as it usually has been—of a locality or a state in which the lumbering or mining industry bulked particularly large, the support of the community or state would flow to the narrow interests of such industry. Some local citizens would be aggrieved at the costs in natural beauty and wilderness but their voices would be so weak in face of the seemingly monolithic determination of their neighbors as to be beneath the threshold of hearing. Indeed, the feeling of powerlessness would generally lead them not to speak at all, given the inevitability of failure and the necessity of living with those neighbors.

Thus, it has generally been true that fights for conservation have taken on an aspect of outsiders against locals. The appearance has been false in that almost any locality contains some individuals concerned for conservation. Nevertheless, these individuals could only be heard in chorus with like-minded fellows drawn from a larger constituency. The exploiters of commodities, understanding the situation at least intuitively, have persistently appealed to the strong American tradition of decentralization as a supposedly democratic principle and have sought to retain the power of decision in local hands. There have been contests in which localities have lined up for conservation, establishment of the Gila Wilderness, for example, but these have been rare. Conservation, and conservation of wilderness and scenic values especially, have depended on creation of larger constituencies. Thus it is not difficult to imagine what would have happened to the Grand Canyon if its future had been left to Arizona to decide instead of the nation; the American people as a whole have a far smaller per capita money stake in damming the canyon's potential kilowatts than do the people of Arizona. It is also understandable why officials of Humboldt County resisted creation of a Redwoods National Park, while a strong

drive for the park came from San Francisco, and why opposition to the North Cascades Park was loudest in Bellingham and Wenatchee and weakest in Seattle.

The change that has come about is far from total. It is in degree only. It is, moreover, a change of some complexity. It involves a new awareness and knowledge of people in New England, the Midwest, and California about the North Cascades, many miles distant from their homes. It involves the increasing urbanization of Americans and the drift of political power to city dwellers. It involves the changing economic base of cities like Seattle, with the relative decline and position of the lumber industry. Thus, it is not inconceivable that the success of the Boeing Company may have been the essential factor in preserving the North Cascades. The change also involves the development of national conservation organizations. All of these have converged in the creation of a larger and more diverse constituency, with a consequently growing power supporting wilderness, scenic values, and environmental protection.

Second, a deep and general change has occurred in our national political life. This is now a rich and prosperous nation. We now have a large generation of youth that has no memory of depression. At long last, we are generally free of the incubus of fear that tomorrow the economy will collapse. This has a very profound meaning—that the substance of political and moral life is no longer almost wholly economic. Economic matters have, in the past, been highly preoccupying, simply because hitherto we have never been out of the shadow of potential famine or other economic disaster. It is highly unlikely that men have ever really believed that economic affairs are the most importa t department of life, but it is true that we have always so far had to give first thought to that department simply because it has had a prior urgency. As a result, our political system has been formulated to adjust economic claims, and it has worked peculiarly well. The reason for this is that economic claims are bargainable; it is almost always possible to split the difference somewhere in an economic contest so that each side is reasonably satisfied. When we respond to the injunction, "Come, let us reason together," it is to bargain and to split differences.

As the nation has become richer, however, economic values have lost their old urgency and other more important matters have emerged and taken the foreground. The values of natural beauty and wilderness are critical examples here. But these are really not bargainable. The sort of "reasoning" which has been characteristic of politics on the economic model does not apply. It is faintly conceivable, for example, that by offering a sufficiently high price to the National Museum in Amsterdam to acquire its treasure, *The Night Watch,* one could get that great painting away from the Dutch; but it is absolutely inconceivable that one could make a deal to get a two-foot square cut out of the lower left-hand quadrant of the picture for *any* price. This is just not a possible bargain.

So it is with supposed bargains offered on natural beauty and wilderness. To bargain over the Grand Canyon, the redwoods, the North Cascades, may seem eminently sensible if you are interested in kilowatts, lumber, or copper, but it is nonetheless immoral if your concern is with scenic beauty and wilderness. Such a bargain might be possible if the value of scenic beauty and wilderness could be stated in the same dollar measure as kilowatts, lumber, and copper. It would,

alternatively, be bargainable if the economic developers were able to offer a new Grand Canyon, some new two-thousand-year-old redwoods, or some new North Cascades in the exchange. Unfortunately, however, this alternative has practical difficulties. The fact of the matter is that any such bargain is completely one-sided—to take away more or less of the Grand Canyon, the redwoods, or the North Cascades. The brute power of the opposition may conceivably win, but such an outcome will not be a bargain in the sense of being mutually acceptable.

This fundamental characteristic of the politics of conservation is deeply involved in what has occurred with the conservation movement. There is much evidence that Americans today have moved beyond the conception that everything of meaning in life can be stated in either dollar or head-count terms. It is evident, for example, that many Americans are willing to go to extreme lengths in their principled opposition to the Viet Nam War. It is plain that many individuals are willing to lay their lives on the line for simple human dignity. And many of our best young people are going to extremes to assert their rejection of the material calculus. Both moral and aesthetic principles are emerging everywhere as the fundamental material of politics and common life. In this setting, increasing numbers of individuals are declaring themselves for what they really believe in. It is hardly surprising that many are declaring the values of scenic beauty and wilderness; there are hardly any values less uncertain and ambiguous than these. Formerly, the sort of ridicule offered by spokesmen for firms such as the Kennecott Copper Corporation, that concern for these values is "sentimental," was effective. We were once half persuaded that such concern was soft-headed, and that these values were inferior. It is beginning to emerge that the really soft-headed sentimentalism is that attaching to money.

The striking evidence of growth in the conservation movement since 1954 is directly related to the clarity with which the conservation leaders of today have perceived the strategic nature of conservation issues. A telling incident on this score is one related to the Echo Park controversy. When the Upper Colorado Project was put forward, nearly everyone believed Echo Park was necessarily doomed. But a small group of individuals got together and decided that the principle involved was simply wrong and that they should say so. This was to be a gesture, but the declaration struck such a chord of public response that ultimately it became possible to save Echo Park by sheer mass support.

The style of the conservation movement is intransigent. It is often shrill and strident. It gives rise to internal controversies of much intensity. However distressing those controversies may be, they are themselves strong evidence of the movement's vitality. They are a measure of the degree to which participants regard their cause as serious. By the same token, today's movement is principled. This very feature is responsible for the great current growth of the conservation movement, and, in fact, is why there is a genuine movement today where there was none before. To the degree that it stands by its principles, it will continue to grow and frequently to succeed. To the degree that it seeks to compromise and make deals, it will fail and wither.

The leaders of the modern conservation movement must expect to be told that they are unreasonable. They must expect continued demands to enter into "bargains" in which they can only lose and never gain. They may be told that they should go back to the old reliable way of quietly finessing things through men of influence. But those days are gone, and with all gratitude to the notable men who managed those coups of influence, their coups cannot now be emulated. Henceforth, the conservation movement will have to succeed as a movement, enduring all the committee meetings, the endless work of organization, and, most of all, hammering out the principles and applications of those principles.

A pioneer in the field of perceptual geography, geographer and historian DAVID LOWENTHAL (b. 1923) brings a variety of disciplines to his study of man's taste in landscape. Frequently his investigations lead into the subconscious, making us aware of things we did not realize about even our own feelings. Do you see how Lowenthal's point, assuming it has validity, challenges some of our basic ideas about environmental management? If Lowenthal was given power to create an outdoor recreation area, what sort of environment would he design?

David Lowenthal

Criteria for Natural Beauty

Early man, according to some of his latter-day descendants, viewed his physical environment with awe and dread. To him, Nature was a tyrant; he survived only by strict obedience to her dictates. To us, it is not Nature but our own creations that are terrifying. Nature seldom threatens most urban Americans; indeed, she scarcely causes us discomfort.

Nevertheless, a new religion of nature is in the making. Worshipers of nature exhort us from the pulpits of countless conservation societies and Audubon clubs; the President's Advisory Commission on Outdoor Recreation transmutes their dogma into national policy; *Life* magazine gives it a four-color im-

primatur. Nature is wonderful, they tell us; pay homage to it in the Wilderness, and where there is no Wilderness, create Open Spaces.

The tone of Senator Wayne Morse's comment on the Wilderness Bill, in 1961, exemplifies the underlying rationale: "You cannot associate with the grandeur of this great heritage which God Almighty has given the American people and not come out of such a trip a better man or woman for having come that close to the spirit of the Creator." Americans are near a state of grace, runs this argument, thanks to their past and present intimacy with the wilderness. Our forefathers mastered a continent; today we celebrate the virtues of the

David Lowenthal, "Not Every Prospect Pleases: What Is Our Criterion for Scenic Beauty?" from Vol. 12:2 of *Landscape* (1962–1963), pp. 19–23.

vanquished foe: To love nature is re- garded as uniquely American. "The out- doors lies deep in American tradition," chants *Outdoor Recreation for America.* "It has had immeasurable impact on the Nation's character and on those who made its history. This is a civilization pain- fully and only recently carved in conflict with the forces of nature . . . When an American looks for the meaning of his past, he seeks it not in ancient ruins, but more likely in mountains and forests, by a river, or at the edge of the sea."

But these are pious sentiments, not historical facts. Our civilization is main- ly imported from Europe, and has had more to contend against in Main Street than in the forests and mountains; pioneer life was usually duller and safer than it is generally imagined; and Americans who seek the meaning of their past look for it in Europe, or in Bunker Hill, Gettysburg, Williamsburg, Free- domland, and the deserted mining towns of the Sierras, precisely because such places are humanized, not wild.

Converts to the wilderness cult, like conservationists generally, tend to feel that their preferences are not only more virtuous than those of others but also more enduring. "Conservation should preserve all the fine things in life. Our heritage must be preserved for those who come after us."—so runs a typical admonition. Long-term or eternal goals are considered ethically superior to im- mediate ones; and future generations are expected to accept present-day pre- cepts about what is important. Yet our great-great-grandchildren may care little for our image of the wilderness. More- over, a heritage cannot be preserved intact; if it were, it would have only anti- quarian interest. Tomorrow's patrimony is bound to be different from today's. The wilderness was no "heritage" to folk who had to cope with it; it became one only when it no longer had to be lived in. The same is true of pastoral land- scapes, rural villages, even of 19th Cen- tury industrial centers; and landscapes now despised will some day be prized as a precious heritage.

The wilderness is not, in fact, a type of landscape at all, but a congeries of feelings about man and nature of vary- ing import to different epochs, cultures and individuals. For Elizabethans, the wilderness was barren, chaotic, frightful, "howling"; for contemporary Europeans, it is often associated with primitive and romantic tribes in distant lands; for many Americans, it is an entity distinct from the workaday world, an oasis where the laws of nature still apply.

The cult of wilderness—its origins and history, its philosophies and programs, its impact on landscapes and its implica- tions for mankind—should receive thorough scrutiny. The way Americans feel about wild nature is intimately bound up, as has been suggested, with this country's special history. But the wilder- ness is only a part of anybody's picture. And attitudes toward wilderness can hardly be understood except in the con- text of beliefs and assumptions concern- ing nature and landscape generally. . . .

Let me discuss some assumptions about the *appearance* of landscape—assump- tions concerning its origins or antiquity, its cultural context or function, and its esthetic congruity. For judgments about the way things ought to look are condi- tioned by how things are thought to have come into being, how old they are, what they are used for, and how well they fit into their surroundings.

Comfortably ensconced in a Pullman car moving through Pennsylvania, the book critic J. Donald Adams saw some- thing from the window "which revolted me, and . . . made me boil with anger. We had been passing through hilly, forested country, still lovely, even in its second growth," writes Adams in his weekly *New York Times* column, "when suddenly I saw a mountain stream so discolored, so noxious as almost to turn one's stomach. It was easy to imagine how it had once looked, sparkling and clear, before the mines somewhere beyond had polluted its waters and made it a thing of blasphemy."

What seems ugly to Adams he condemns as evil; but which of these judgments determined the other? He cannot be certain that the stream is polluted—he is no hydrologist. Suppose he learned the water was discolored not by mining but by a sulfur vent upstream, or simply by turbid spring floods; would he still find it "noxious"? If he knew nature were responsible for the color of the stream, would he "boil with anger"? Would he still conjure up an image of pristine purity? In short, Adams takes it for granted that landscapes he enjoys are natural, and that those he dislikes have been ruined by man. Nature beautifies; man deforms. To alter the natural order is inherently wicked and *hence* displeasing to the eye. The forest, like the stream, is judged by this dictum. "Still lovely, *even* in its second growth," the wooded hillside is more attractive than some denuded slope, but lacks the perfection of the primitive forest.

Where landscapes are not patently marred by man, it is all too easy to assume that they are primeval. To the city dweller, anything that is not geometrically arranged may seem in the realm of untouched nature. He seldom distinguishes the pastoral from the wild. Indeed, in a landscape seen for the first time every component—mountains, old houses, even billboards—is apt to strike the viewer as a durable fixture of the scene.

But no matter how natural or untouched they may look, most landscapes have been profoundly altered by man, directly or indirectly, over long periods of time. "A field of pasture grass looks as if it had been there forever," remarks Edward Hyams, "and it is hard to absorb the fact that, like any urban square, it has been imposed on the wild." One intuitively feels that if man had interfered with the lovely vista it would bear obvious marks of manufacture, alteration or decay. "Surely a water-meadow, with its lush grass knee-high to the cows and its decoration of tall golden buttercups . . . is a gift of God, or nature." Not so; "we owe it all to the greed for gain of a speculating 17th Century nobleman and the engineering skill of some Dutch drainage expert." On the other hand, some aspects of nature seem artificial. Vegetation is apt to look more "natural" than barren rock, because we perceive analogies between geological and architectural structures—many tourists, asserts Joseph Wood Krutch, assume the Grand Canyon is at least partly man-made.

Misconceptions about man's role in landscape formation are universal and probably inevitable. Appearances lead people in all cultures and eras to assume that some things are "manmade," others natural, when the truth would reveal the opposite, or more likely an intermingling of agencies. What is unusual—and, to my mind, destructive—is to combine wrong notions of landscape genesis with the moral judgment that men generally act for mean motives and with effects offensive to the sight.

The contemporary tendency to find beauty and good in the "natural," ugliness or squalor in what man dominates is not only moralistic; it is an esthetic aberration in the history of landscape taste. The contrary view has usually prevailed. Thus to Daniel Defoe, Westmoreland was "the wildest, most barren and frightful" county in England: he liked nothing about it except "some pleasant manufacturing towns." In most canons of landscape beauty, man and his works occupy a prominent place. A century and a half ago, in a fairly representative view, Arthur Young described the clang and smoke and flames of the iron forges at Colebrook Dale as "altogether sublime." Russians today similarly admire Kochegarka mine, the "pride" of Gorlovka with its magnificent slag heaps scattered over the steppe for miles around.

By and large, men find lived-in landscapes more attractive than wild ones. "We have in places made the Earth more beautiful than it was before we came," Sir Francis Younghusband maintained in his Royal Geographical Society address: "I can realize what the river-valleys of England must have been like before the arrival of man—beautiful, certainly; but not *so* beautiful as now. . . . Now the marshes are drained and turned into golden meadows. The woods are cleared in part and well-kept parks take their place. . . . And homes are built . . . which in the setting of trees and lawns and gardens add unquestionably to the natural beauty of the land."

Raw nature was condemned also by 19th Century Americans. The Rockies and the Sierras displeased early tourists. "The dreariness of the desolate peak itself scarcely dissipates the dismal spell," one traveler wrote of Pike's Peak, "for you stand in a hopeless confusion of dull stones piled upon each other in odious ugliness." Americans preferred the picturesque—caverns evocative of cathedrals, pillars resembling ruined castles. If they could not have real ruins, they wanted make-believe ones; they had had a plethora of wilderness. To admire, much less love, wild nature, as Daniel Beard advocated, initially seemed ludicrous to almost everyone. Indeed, the first forest reserves were called "primitive areas" because according to Earl Pomeroy, the government feared "the public might find the word 'wilderness' repulsive."

All that is changed; for contemporary Americans, it is civilization that is hard to endure. A "primitive area" is now a place, according to the Outdoor Recreation Resources Review Commission, in which one enjoys a "wilderness experience"—"a sense of being so far removed from the sights and sounds of civilization that he is alone with nature." The implications of this statement underlie most of the issues I have raised. Are the "sights and sounds" of civilization more difficult to live with than those of nature? Is being alone with nature the only, or even the best, alternative to civilization? What about being alone in rural or pastoral countrysides, or in landscapes full of historic ruins but void of present day activity? And how much do these distinctions matter if one is not aware of them? Consider an urbanite walking in woods where human enterprise is apparent to any Indian or woodsman, but invisible to him; does he not feel as alone with nature as he would in a truly primeval landscape? Alternatively, if J. Donald Adams suspected the green on leaves came from manufactured chlorophyll, would he not find the forest ugly? Oranges look unnatural only when we are told their color is artificial.

Few Americans, however, are devotees exclusively of the aboriginal; many are fond of the merely old. Landscapes that cannot qualify as pure wilderness may still be acceptable if they are sufficiently ancient, uncontaminated by contemporary life, or relics of an epoch when (it is assumed) man lived in harmony with his surroundings. Americans tout no particular era as an acme of esthetic virtue; all they ask is certified antiquity, preferably numerically precise. It is the anachronistic appearance that is all-important. Critics of Malraux's clean-up program for the *monuments historiques* of Paris protest that rejuvenation "has robbed them of their weight of reality, that the Concorde palaces now look like Hollywood movie sets of the Concorde palaces." And the Hotel Crillon rejected cleaning outright because, noted Genêt in the *New Yorker,* "its clientele, especially the Americans, had faith in the dirt of the facade as a guarantee that they were living in a geniunely historic old place." Few people are really taken in by such a "guarantee." But this matters little; . . . we are willing to be fooled even when we know we are being fooled.

At home, visual self-deception is unabashed. Dirt is all right on European facades; here, it is matter out of place. For every restored Williamsburg, there are countless generic prototypes like Old Sturbridge Village—sanitary facsimiles rather than actual places, which rely for verisimilitude on scholarly precision. Self-conscious and sentimental about the past, we fence it off in special landscapes of its own, as if history were a zoo. Repair jobs for Niagara Falls and other "natural" scenic wonders are deemed proper because they preserve or restore nature's creations; artifice is the means, not the end. But even where entirely new effects are produced, as with floodlights in caves or music piped out of scenery, the landscape passes for "natural" as long as the face of the earth is not grossly and visibly altered. In the classic phrase of a Long Island developer, "We don't tamper with nature . . . we improve upon it!"

What Americans see in landscapes, and how well they like them, depend also on how the landscapes are being used. Form is supposed to fit function; camouflage is arty and dishonest. We like to call a spade a spade: however ugly a factory, a city dump, a used-car lot may seem to the passerby, as long as it fulfills its function it is presumed to look all right. If the used-car dealer didn't like the way his lot looked, he'd do something about it—not for his own visual pleasure, to be sure, but to attract customers. To enjoy a landscape or to commune with nature, we go to the wilderness. We do not prettify the rugged face of workaday America.

The landscape, in short, is worthy of its hire. Its ultimate critics are its residents, not its visitors, however unappreciative the former, however learned or perceptive the latter. This is the burden of a passage in William James's "On a Certain Sense of Blindness in Human Beings":

"Journeying in the mountains of North Carolina, I passed by a large number of 'coves,' . . . which had been newly cleared and planted. The impression on my mind was one of unmitigated squalor. The settler had in every case cut down the more manageable trees, and left their charred stumps standing. The larger trees he had girdled and killed . . . and had set up a tall zigzag rail fence around the scene of his havoc, to keep the pigs and cattle out. Finally, he had irregularly planted the intervals between the stumps and trees with Indian corn. . . . The forest had been destroyed; and what had 'improved' it out of existence was hideous, a sort of ulcer, without a single element of artificial grace to make up for the loss of Nature's beauty. . . . Talk about going back to Nature! I said to myself, oppressed by the dreariness. . . . No modern person ought to be willing to live a day in such a state of rudimentariness and denudation."

Then a mountaineer told James, "'Why, we ain't happy here, unless we are getting one of these coves under cultivation.'"

"I instantly felt that I had been losing the whole inward significance of the situation. . . . To me the clearings spoke of naught but denudation. . . . But, when *they* looked on the hideous stumps, what they thought of was personal victory. The chips, the girdled trees, and the vile split rails spoke of honest sweat, persistent toil and final reward. . . . In short, the clearing, which to me was a mere ugly picture on the retina, was to them a symbol redolent with moral memories and sang a very paean of duty, struggle and success."

And he points the moral: "The spectator's judgment is sure to miss the root of the matter, and to possess no truth."

James considers the mountaineers' impression truer and nobler than his own, not because they see better, but because they have a better right to judge. Beauty is in the eye of the beholder, to be sure; but which beholder is right? Why, the man who is usually on the spot—presumably the shepherd on the Downs, the sexton at St. Paul's, the elevator operator in the Eiffel Tower. He may have no time, training, or inclination for an esthetic appreciation of landscape; no matter, he acquires it by osmosis.

Preoccupation with purpose is in fact no aid, but a deterrent to landscape appreciation. The man who has to consider what things are used for is least likely to note their shapes, colors and patterns. To exalt his judgment is to promote a complacent inattention to appearance, an abnegation of esthetic response. The visitor's view is discounted,

but the resident is too preoccupied to have a view.

There are a few who care, or pretend to care, about the way things look where they live. But many homeowners are satisfied by linguistic landscaping. Through emotive names—even by such geographical fantasies as Hilldale Heights, Valmont Gardens, and Glencrest Homes—"an idealized landscape is imposed on an existing one by verbal *force majeure,*" as Arthur Minton points out in *Names.* Maybe only God can make a tree, but any real-estate developer can create a veritable forest in the mind's eyes of his clients.

Few people really look at the places they live in, work in, or travel through. Anesthetized against their surroundings, they spare themselves pain. "Start by looking at things, and then one becomes aware how hideous they really are," writes F. F. C. Curtis in the *Journal of the Royal Society of Arts.* "Some towns are hideous from one end to the other. I think it is because people do not open their eyes and do not recognize them as hideous."

The concept of scenic beauty, formerly tied to specific attributes, has since the 18th Century lost all precise meaning; it now promiscuously denotes anything that gives pleasure. "We talk about a 'sublime' or 'lovely' landscape," as Fenichel says, "because we feel sublime or lovely when seeing a landscape of this kind." No longer captives of the picturesque, we do not require that scenery look like a painting; and we can enjoy landscapes that point no meaning or moral.

Nonetheless, certain landscapes look right, others wrong or unhappily composed. They may seem incongruous because we have a pictorial bias against certain combinations of form and color, or a teleological outlook that condemns assemblages unless they look planned. Some of us find landscapes deformed unless the visual assemblage is familiar. Various objects, shapes or colors may seem out of place in certain settings. The totally strange and new may be less unsettling than a combination of known with unknown elements, or of forms belonging to two or more disparate cultural contexts. Those used to Western European or North American landscapes find something absurd and dissonant in lands where mules coexist with motorcars, and temperate zone flowers compete with tropical vegetation. The commingling of familiar and exotic, or of past and present, can be bizarre and disturbing.

Whatever the reason, most people expect a measure of visual harmony in landscapes. But the measure is personal as well as cultural: variety pleasing to one individual may pass unnoticed by a second and seem a shocking mélange to a third. Take litter. Most Americans pile junk in town dumps and automobile graveyards or throw it in rivers and down railway embankments. But streets and the countryside generally are free of cans and paper—otherwise, someone complains.

Other cultures treat litter differently. From an apartment in one tropical land I recently looked out at a garden, a stretch of grass that passed as lawn and pleasant buildings opposite. What made the scene seem so tawdry? Garden and lawn were strewn with paper and cans. Litter collected there, months on end, because *no one saw it;* to the residents, cans and paper did not seem out of place among grass and flowers. And to many folk, here as well as abroad, cans and paper are not litter at all, but valuable materials for construction and fuel.

The problem is made evident and vivid when litter is mistaken for something view-worthy. Disillusioned by mistaking a piece of blue paper on a hillside for a flower, A. M. Sayers asks in the *New Statesman,* "*Why* do we dislike litter? . . . Is the disgust rooted in fear of one's fellows as a whole? No Ancient Roman or medieval 'litter' doesn't trouble us. . . . Is it to do with the Age of Paper? Why should amphorae be so much more respectable than old tin cans?" But some people see nothing disreputable in old tin cans. Everything depends on what is considered "out of place," on the rate of decay, on how rapidly artifacts cease to be junk and become part of the heritage. And these are matters of great complexity. . . . What makes one landscape appear harmonious, another incongruous, is the entire experience of the viewer.

Like Alan Trachtenberg, RICHARD G. LILLARD (b. 1909) explores a microcosm and emerges with information relevant to the whole experience of Americans with the environment. In this case Lillard focuses on the advent of the age of automobiles in Yosemite National Park. His discussion soon broadens to a far-reaching examination of the purposes of parks and nature preservation generally. What do you think the order of priorities should be in national parks? Man, then nature, or nature and then man? Be aware that your answers may offend many of the "owners" of these public places.

Richard G. Lillard

Priorities in Nature Preservation

One of the important questions now before us is the question of the admission of automobiles to national parks and the terms upon which they should be admitted if they are to be admitted, either to this park or to any other park". This crucial, incisive remark was made in Yosemite Valley by Secretary of the Interior Walter L. Fisher on October 14, 1912. The occasion was the second National Park Conference, attended by dozens of important persons from coast to coast: representatives of the American Civic Association: national forest and park officials, including Clement S. Ucker, chief clerk of the Interior Department: hotel, stagecoach, and railroad men, including F. F. Harvey, manager of dining-car service on the Santa Fe Railway. Many Californians were present: Frank Miller of Riverside Mission Inn; Yosemite concessionaires like David Curry: businessmen from nearby mountain towns: big-city automobile dealers, and leaders of the several automobile associations. Conservationists were among them—notably John Muir, author of magazine articles that had made Yosemite famous, and William E. Colby, his heir apparent, secretary of the Sierra Club.

The conference came about after years of agitation by individual automobile owners and their spokesmen to get machines admitted to Yosemite Valley, that prestigious little glacial slot in the

Reprinted by permission of the publisher. "The Siege and Conquest of a National Park," *The American West,* January, 1968. American West Publishing Company, Palo Alto, California. Pp. 28–31, 67, 69–71.

Sierra Nevada, that colossal exhibit of granite domes and misty waterfalls, that *Ahwahnee* or "deep grassy place" of the Indians, with more square miles to its sides than to its level bottom. In 1912 this climactic example of "America the Beautiful" was hard to reach and taboo to cars. The conferees had approached the Valley in private automobiles or by railroad, but they entered it in buggies, stagecoaches, or motor stages based in the Valley. By government edict all three of the one-lane privately owned access roads were closed to automobiles.

Doughnut-shaped Yosemite National Park had been created in 1890, around the state-owned Yosemite Valley, which had been added in 1906 to plug the hole. It was as large as Rhode Island, but all the pressure then as now was to get into the sacred inner citadel—the Valley itself—only seven miles long and always less than a mile wide, smaller than the total area of some modern airports.

It was at this conference that the automobile issue was most lengthily discussed, and the decision was more or less made to let automobiles in. Men spoke with self-assumed prophetic powers about automobiles—for the history of the automobile lay ahead. But the conference came a year before any automobiles got in and years before the rise of a traffic problem that is increasingly unsolved. It came when neither California nor the federal government had any road-building programs, before there was a highway contractors' lobby, before there were any large automobile corporations, even before there was any national parks agency.

The conference of 1912 remains central and symbolic in national park and conservation history, for the arguments over Yosemite Valley were arguments over the locale that had generated the national park idea in the 1860's.* The Valley had become the first great showplace of the great West, ranking with the veteran American attractions of Niagara Falls, the Hudson River Gorge, the Natural Bridge of Virginia, and Mammoth Cave—none of which embodied such a variety of features, gigantic or delicate. And the conference was held just as Americans were beginning to respond to the slogan "See America First"; just when transcontinental automobile travel by ordinary people was about to start; when private organizations would boost routes with such enthralling names as "The Ocean to Ocean Highway"; when the completion of the Panama Canal would focus attention on the Pacific Coast and occasion the Panama-California Exposition in San Diego and the Panama-Pacific International Exposition in San Francisco.

Already a few autoists had been allowed access to Mount Rainier, Crater Lake, and General Grant national parks, under severe local rules, but there was no uniform federal policy on the question or any assurance that cars would continue to be allowed in. The arguments over Yosemite and the ultimate decision to let the horseless bourgeois carriages into the aristocratic Sierran Troy opened a new chapter in the relations between mankind and special areas of natural beauty. The "touring craze" was to change the character of the Valley, as it was to alter the face of America.

Secretary Fisher, who opened the conference briskly and kept it moving, was aware that knowingly or not the group assembled there faced key issues of the twentieth century—issues of progress, mechanization, democracy, aesthetic values, automotive values, recreational

---

*See the discussion above, pp. 29–31.—Ed.

values, and economic power, Fisher was a lean, astute Illinois lawyer, a civic-minded enemy of "gray wolves" (corrupt Chicago aldermen), a former traction counsel for Chicago, former president of the National Conservation League, a superb cross-examiner of witnesses, a nimble speaker, and a martinet of a chairman. A year before, in Yellowstone, he had presided at a conference that took up many topics, but he knew that this time the topic of obsessive proportions was the internal combustion engine.

He knew of the files of mail and the duplicate telegrams from auto partisans that had accumulated for months in the files in Washington. He knew the automobilists' standard arguments and the conservationists' replies. He said the automobiles would eventually get in, and he wanted to be down-to-earth and "talk man-fashion" about the proper conditions for admitting them. Like a good administrator, rather than a good politician, he wanted constructive, specific suggestions. . . .

John B. Curtin of Sonara, a Democratic state senator, one of the owners of the Big Oak Flat Road, and strictly a businessman, wanted the Valley opened up because it was one of the nation's assets to exploit. A child of nineteenth-century optimism, with rationalization if not faith or reason, Senator Curtin said:

I am one of those people who believe in modern progress and that each condition which arises will take care of itself, and the only thing we can do is to endeavor to minimize danger in all walks of life. . . . Then go into the valley with the automobile and don't let the horse keep it out. The automobile is the new business and the horse is the old one—that is the point I want to make. . . . My friend spoke of Christ riding a jackass through Jerusalem. I do not believe he would have done it if he had had an automobile. I want

to say . . . that I am one of those people who believe in modern progress.

William Colby, speaking for the Sierra Club—which was founded to save Yosemite—said of the autoists: "We hope they will be able to come in when the time comes, because we think the automobile adds a great zest to travel and we are primarily interested in the increase of travel to these parks." Secretary Fisher, who said that "a very strong sentiment exists in many quarters against having automobiles admitted to the Yosemite Valley," asked Colby if the proper time had come. "I think it is very close at hand," said Colby. He was for letting cars drive along the rim to Glacier Point and for improving the road from Inspiration Point down. He saw no harm in mixing cars and horses. The mountain roads were no different from Market Street. . . .

Later in 1912, at a banquet of the American Civic Association in Baltimore, . . . James Bryce, the British Ambassador to the United States, spoke with wisdom and prescience about the need to create national parks and remember what they are for: "With your great population and the growing desire to enjoy the beauties of Nature, you do not have any more than you need." In one long passage he advised Americans to keep the parks, specifically Yosemite, in good condition.

If Adam had known what harm the serpent was going to work, he would have tried to prevent him from finding lodgment in Eden; and if you were to realize what the result of the automobile will be in that wonderful, that incomparable valley, you will keep it out. The automobile means dust, it moves too fast and interferes with detailed esthetic enjoyment, it prevents contemplation, it destroys the whole feeling of the spontaneity and freshness of primitive nature.

After reading both Colby's testimony at Yosemite and Bryce's address at Baltimore, the Massachusetts forester and conservationist, G. Frederick Schwarz, wrote Colby. He said he was surprised that Colby and Muir would admit cars into the Valley "when the time comes," a time that "is very close at hand." Even allowing that automobiles will evolve, said Schwarz, and become more quiet, smoother-running, and perhaps odorless, such machinery would be artificial and out of place in any of the parks, with "the wonderful charm of their great, brooding quietness." It would destroy their "*necessary* characteristics."

Colby quickly replied, saying that "this matter has received careful thought and consideration by both Mr. Muir and myself." He gave three arguments. First, automobiles mean a tremendous increase in travel and larger congressional appropriations. Second, horses would be relieved of the strain of pulling stages, which rapidly cripples and exhausts them. Electric lines could not be thought of, for their ugly poles and tracks were constantly in sight. Third, Colby saw the automobile as a new force in civilization, "with tremendous impetus" and "irresistible force and reason behind its use." Therefore, opposing it would weaken the conservationist cause and "give our detractors the opportunity of calling us visionary, fakirs, etc."

Schwarz wrote back to suggest that it would not work for long to let cars in and expect them to stay immobile. He cited destructive changes he had seen in England's New Forest and on old Cape Cod in Massachusetts. "My experience has been that automobiles, notwithstanding their many practical advantages, soon change the character of a locality." He had no argument, he said, to meet Colby's contentions that the car had an irresistible

power to establish itself. He could only hope for the best. . . .

On March 4 [1913] . . . Fisher left office, along with Taft and conservation, and Franklin K. Lane, an important member of the Interstate Commerce Commission, became Secretary of the Interior under Woodrow Wilson and the New Freedom. Since Lane was a Californian and a liberal, practical politician, he was expected to sympathize with "this right of the automobilists" to enter the forbidden valley. As Lane delayed the fateful announcement . . . the letters continued to come, some for ingress to a "playground" and others for protection of "the primeval beauty and grandeur of the ancient days of our beloved country.". . .

On April 30 came his literary "Memorandum for the Press," which got one inch in the *New York Times* but shook the western automotive world. "I have decided to allow automobiles to enter the Yosemite Valley," he wrote. "This form of transportation has come to stay and to close the Valley against automobiles would be as absurd as the fight for many years made by old naval men against the adoption of steam in the Navy. Before we know it, they will be dropping into the Yosemite by airship." (The first plane landed in 1919.) . . . His final point echoed the autoists' thesis and forecast what was to happen in the Valley: "I want to make our parks as accessible as possible to the great mass of people."

"Autoists Exult over Victory in Yosemite Fight," cried the *San Francisco Examiner*. "The triumph for the Motor Car Dealers Association is in keeping with the record being made by this State as the greatest user of automobiles in the world." Lane had given "motor-car owners their rights" and kept pace "with modern progress." The California Automobile Association and the Automobile Club of Southern California each also claimed the victory. But not until printed entrance forms had arrived in the Valley on August 23, after a delay that irritated eager victors, did the Park actually open to cars. By October 1 a total of 127 cars had entered. . . .

In 1914, 739 cars entered the Park; in 1915, 2,270; in 1916, 4,043; in 1917, 6,521; in 1918, despite the war, 7,621; in 1928, after the All-Year Road had opened the Park to one and all, anytime, 136,689 cars.

Meanwhile, people continued to praise and blame the automobile, often in almost adjacent sentences. In 1921, in his *Yosemite and Its High Sierra*, John H. Williams said, "The most effective step yet taken to make the National Park of practical use to the people was the admission of private automobiles," and also Yosemite Valley is "in grave danger of speedily becoming the most overcrowded tourist center in America." Stephen T. Mather, the borax executive who became the first director of the National Park Service [1917–1929], and whose job was created by the attention that automobiles had brought to the parks, was himself an "auto crank" and loved to drive his own Packard. He once urged D. J. Desmond, a new concessionaire and organizer of the Yosemite National Park Company, to build a hotel in the Valley. Desmond foresaw empty rooms and bankruptcy. Mather exclaimed: "Why, look at those cars! There must be close to two hundred of them. Where's your imagination, man? Some day there'll be a thousand." Desmond said, "Maybe."

At the National Park Conference in Yellowstone in 1911 a landscape architect and planner had asked for a definition of the function of national parks, and no one had given an answer. Five years later the "Act to Establish a National Park Service" clearly said that

. . . the fundamental purpose of the said parks, monuments and reservations . . . is to conserve the scenery and the natural and historic objects and the wild life therein and to provide for the enjoyment of the same in such manner and by such means as will leave them unimpaired for the enjoyment of future generations.

This statement helped, and now Mather and his assistants Horace Albright and Robert Yard composed a definition for their own use: "areas of unmodified natural conditions, each the finest of its type in the country, preserved forever as a system from all industrial uses." Involved were educational values and superlative landscape, which fitted hand and glove. But also involved was the internal contradiction in the Act of 1916 between the ideal of preservation and the idea of use—a contradiction that no one much saw then, just as no one much saw that each running engine is a kind of industrial use. Secretary Lane himself, honest and goodhearted, believed in exploitation of resources. It was he who resolutely gave Hetch Hetchy to San Francisco,* violating the park. He and his associates were patriotic Americans and western boosters who saw national parks as bringing in carloads of potential settlers and investors. Lane admired the American pioneer. In *Fruits of Faith* he said, "To conquer nature man broke down the gates of the Garden of Eden and came forth to meet the challenge of an unadorned world."

The policies of wide-open gates that Lane and Mather set lead to the present. Since the end of World War II the number of cars per year have passed the half-million mark and kept increasing. Bigger

*See the account below, pp. 71–74.—Ed.

and bigger urban crowds are less and less interested in seeing nature or hiking, more and more interested in sunbathing, beer-drinking, dancing, nibbling between meals, shopping, and watching entertainment. Pine groves and apple orchards and meadows give way to parking lots. Campgrounds become densely populated, one-story tenements not unlike Arab refugee camps. On summer weekends, off-limits parked cars, people, and litter are everywhere. Millions of feet trample riverbanks into loose rubble, meadows into packed brown dirt. Traffic roars twenty-four hours a day, echoing from the mighty cliffs of El Capitan and Glacier Point. Truck drivers gun their engines. Motorcycles sputter at all hours. At the highway entrances traffic slows to a crawl or stops, and at 9 P.M. the autoists who push along the open meadows to see a stunt called the "fire fall"* immobilize the Valley road loops. The Valley that Greeley and Emerson, Grant and Garfield endured long coach rides to see, that Bierstadt and Moran crossed the continent to paint, that Ansel Adams has photographed magnificently by tilting his camera up from or away from the people and cars—this Valley is now "incomparable" as an exhibit of ecological imbalance. There are too many people for the water supply, too many gallons of sewage for the earth to hold, too many campers for the wood supply, too many fishermen for the fish, too many vehicles for the terrain. There are so many thousands of campfires and commercial kitchens, and idling engines and gaseous exhaust pipes, that the atmosphere grows misty and smoggy.

Only the concessionaires are happy,

selling food and trinkets in their shops and supermarkets to daily populations of forty to fifty thousand persons, and pumping more gasoline per day than there is water in Mirror Lake in August. There has even been serious talk of putting up high-rise hotels to house the visitors, as at the southern end of Lake Tahoe.

In the 1940's and 1950's Bernard DeVoto was sounding warnings in *Harper's* and *The Saturday Evening Post*. "Shall We Let Them Ruin Our National Parks?" In 1961 Professor John Ise prefaced his scholarly, factual *Our National Park Policy* with statements of personal dismay about impossible parking at Old Faithful, lines of sputtering cars in Zion Canyon, and the Yosemite Valley that was "almost an overcrowded slum." Ise said that "our population explosion and the ubiquitous automobile . . . are turning our fair land into a madhouse."

In 1966 articles in *Forbes Magazine*, the *Los Angeles Times*, and other periodicals were pointing up the automobile and attendant phenomena that made Yosemite Valley an issue of continental significance. The *Wall Street Journal* gave featured space to

AH, WILDERNESS
SEVERE OVERCROWDING
BRINGS ILLS OF THE CITY
TO SCENIC YOSEMITE
PARK'S RANGERS FIGHT CRIME,
TRAFFIC JAMS, SMOG; BEARS
BECOME SURLY GOURMANDS
OTHER PARKS THREATENED, TOO

One park official was quoted as saying, "It's automobiles, not people, that are crowding the parks." Another said, "The valley is too fragile for the treatment it's been getting. Within a few years we'll have to outlaw both camping and automobiles here." The assistant postmaster said,

---

*Since Lillard wrote this event has been eliminated by order of Yosemite's Superintendent as part of a policy of revising the trend described here. — Ed.

"The whole damn valley will be black-topped soon."

From 1913 to 1966—in little more than half a century the automobile had proved its power. No one now needed to prophesy about it, for it had five decades of history to flaunt. It had brought more downgrading changes to Yosemite Valley than the previous five thousand years of erosion. Each day it was cramming a medium-sized city into a valley meant for a hamlet.

Responsible people are faced again with big questions. What is progress, if there is such a thing? Where do automobile values stop and other values begin? Can we longer endure having the NPS become the National Parking System? When and where does the government say "No" to the car? How much vested—and invested—interest does a concessionaire have? What about democracy and the alleged right to unlimited access? When is a tourist attraction "full"? What can be learned from the Alpine Europeans about inconspicuous scenic electric trains and aerial tramways? Why not immediately take steps to disassociate national parks from the playground idea? Does the present federal campaign to keep Americans in America and seeing their own country mean travel only to see other travelers traveling or creep-ing in low gear to campgrounds and tarpaulin resorts already crammed tight?

What can the authorities do to apply the National Park Act of 1916 to Yosemite Valley, once again setting a precedent for other parks? Put the cars back on the rim, outside the park? Bring in the army again, to the constructive peacetime task of enforcing rules that civilians and their officials endlessly ignore, violate, or alter? Dismantle the "improvements" and give nature several centuries to recover? Charge high entrance fees? Require all visitors to write ahead for reservations, as California does for trips through Hearst's Castle at San Simeon, a state park? Go back to one-way roads and stagecoaches, regaining charm and adventure as in the careful historical reconstructions at Sturbridge, Massachusetts, and Williamsburg, Virginia?

The ironies in the victory of the autoists of 1913 are now clear to some of the millions of today's automobile owners. The words of Forester Schwarz and Ambassador Bryce are still with us. "My experience has been that automobiles, notwithstanding their many practical advantages, soon change the character of a locality." . . . "If you were to realize what the result of the automobile will be in that wonderful, that incomparable valley, you will keep it out."

The pioneer and ecological perspectives on the environment are clearly poles apart. But RODERICK NASH (b. 1939) of the University of California, Santa Barbara here shows how the utilitarian and aesthetic emphasis *within* American conservation could also come into sharp conflict. Nash has set the conservation schism in its broader historical context in *Wilderness and the American Mind.*

Roderick Nash

The Conservation Schism

In March, 1868, a self-styled "poetico-trampo-geologist-bot. and ornith-natural, etc!-!-!-!" named John Muir arrived in San Francisco and, allegedly, immediately asked to be shown "any place that is wild." His search took him into the Sierra, and in the following decades Muir became the leading interpreter of these mountains as well as America's foremost publicizer of wilderness values in general. Three years after Muir came West, another young man, fleeing the great Chicago fire, arrived in California. William Kent also sought the wilderness—to such an extent that he could state without much exaggeration: "My life has been largely spent outdoors." Independently

wealthy and of a reforming temperament, Kent pursued a political career in which conservation played a major part. Inevitably his trail crossed Muir's. Indeed in 1908 Kent insisted that the tract of virgin redwood forest he gave to the public be called the Muir Woods National Monument. But in the next five years San Francisco's attempt to secure the Hetch Hetchy Valley in Yosemite National Park as a reservoir site created an issue that caused a major schism among conservationists. The friendship of John Muir and William Kent was one of the casualties of the Hetch Hetchy fight. Faced with the need to choose between different definitions of "conservation," they ended in

Reprinted from *Pacific Historical Review,* Nov. 1967, "John Muir, William Kent, and the Conservative Schism," pp. 423–433, Vol. 34, by permission of the Regents of The University of California. Footnotes omitted.

opposing camps, learning that in regard to conservation the most intense conflicts are often family affairs.

Rising north of the Golden Gate in Marin County, Mt. Tamalpais dominates San Francisco Bay, and its western slope affords a favorable environment for the towering coast redwood and a lush understory of alder, laurel, and fern. William Kent's home was near Tamalpais, and in 1903 it came to his attention that one of its last unlogged canyons was for sale. Kent knew the area and confessed that "the beauty of the place attracted me, and got on my mind, and I could not forget the situation." But the $45,000 asking price was formidable even for Kent. Still, when his wife protested, he simply asked: "If we lost all the money we have and saved those trees it would be worthwhile, wouldn't it?" The purchase of almost three hundred acres in Redwood Canyon followed. Kent had hopes of "a wilderness park for San Francisco and the Bay Cities." Commenting in September, 1903, on the plan, he explained that "whatever occupation man may follow, there is planted within him a need of nature, calling . . . to him at times to come and . . . seek recuperation and strength." Crowded cities, he added, produced "physical, moral, and civic degradation" and, at the same time, the need to escape to wilder environments.

With this attitude John Muir was in full sympathy. "Civilized man chokes his soul," he noted in 1871, "as the heathen Chinese their feet." He believed that centuries of primitive existence had implanted in human nature a yearning for adventure, freedom, and contact with nature which city life could not satisfy. Deny this urge, and the thwarted longings produced tension and despair; indulge it periodically in the wilderness, and there was both mental and physical reinvigoration. Steeped as he was in Transcendentalism, Muir never doubted that nature was a "window opening into heaven, a mirror reflecting the Creator." And *wild* nature, he believed, provided the best "conductor of divinity" because it was least associated with man's artificial constructs. Summing up his philosophy, Muir declared: "In God's wildness lies the hope of the world —the great fresh, unblighted, unredeemed wilderness."

Like Kent, Muir recognized the necessity of the formal preservation of wild country if future generations were to have any left. In 1890 he was a prime mover in the establishment of Yosemite National Park. Two years later he became president of the Sierra Club, an organization dedicated to wilderness enjoyment and preservation. After the turn of the century Muir emerged as a major figure in both the nature-writing genre and the conservation movement.

In 1907 William Kent returned to Marin County from a Hawaiian vacation to find that the North Coast Water Company was beginning condemnation proceedings against his land in Redwood Canyon for the purpose of creating a reservoir. Convinced that wilderness preservation took precedence over private development of water resources, Kent searched for a way of obtaining permanent protection for the area. When the Antiquities Act of 1906 came to his attention, he recognized its possibilities at once. The statute enabled the president to issue executive orders designating tracts of land in the public domain with exceptional historical or natural interest as national monuments. The federal government might also accept gifts of private land for this purpose. Taking the act at its word, in December, 1907, Kent informed Chief Forester Gifford Pinchot and Secretary of the Interior James R.

Garfield that he wished to give Redwood Canyon to the government. Photographs and descriptions of the trees, some of the latter by John Muir, accompanied the application. Kent himself described the area as "the most attractive bit of wilderness I have ever seen."

A final draft of the deed went to Secretary Garfield on December 26, and on January 9, 1908, President Theodore Roosevelt proclaimed the land a national monument. Naming the monument proved more complicated. Although he did not know Muir personally, Kent had long admired him as an interpreter of wilderness values and determined to name the reserve in his honor. But late in January he received a letter from the president asking permission to use "Kent" in its title. Kent responded on January 30, thanking Roosevelt for the proclamation and encouragement in saving "more of the precious and vanishing glories of nature for a people too slow of perception." But Kent refused to accept the change in name. If his sons could not keep the family name alive, he was willing it should be forgotten. When Roosevelt conceded "By George! You are right," the designation Muir Woods National Monument was confirmed.

The wide publicity Kent received for his philanthropy pleased him on several counts. In the first place the land involved was still subject to condemnation; Kent wanted an aroused public opinion on his side. Second, his political ambitions, which carried him to the House of Representatives in 1910, were beginning to stir, and "conservation" was a potent, if vaguely defined, word in the Progressive vocabulary. The attention accorded Kent the donor of Muir Woods could not fail to help Kent the candidate. And praise poured in from all sides. *Sunset, Collier's,* and the *Sierra Club Bulletin* ran illus-trated articles on the new national monument while newspapers throughout the country picked up the story. The Sierra Club made Kent an honorary member, and in June, 1908, Yale awarded him an honorary Master of Arts. Meanwhile, Kent received numerous congratulatory letters applauding him for upholding esthetic and spiritual qualities in a materialistic age.

Kent's gift and personal tribute deeply touched John Muir. On the day Roosevelt created the monument, Muir wrote that in view of the "multitude of dull money hunters" usually associated with undeveloped land, it was "refreshing" to find someone like Kent. Five days later he wrote Kent personally, calling Muir Woods "the finest forest and park thing done in California in many a day." "How it shines," Muir enthused, "amid the mean commercialism and apathy so destructively prevalent these days." Early in February he again thanked Kent for "the best tree-lover's monument that could be found in all the forests of the world." Protecting the redwoods, in Muir's view, was "a much needed lesson to saint and sinner alike, and a credit and encouragement to God." It astonished Muir that "so fine divine a thing should have come out of money-mad Chicago" and he ended by wishing Kent "immortal Sequoia life."

The three years following the establishment of Muir Woods National Monument marked the zenith in the relationship of Kent and Muir. They even discussed the possibility of collaborating in "the general cause of nature preservation." But friction was already mounting within the conservation movement. Those who would preserve undeveloped land for its esthetic, spiritual, and recreational values as wilderness found themselves opposed to resource managers with plans for efficiently harvesting nature's bounties.

In the fall of 1897 Muir abandoned his efforts to support professional forestry and, as a consequence, feuded with Gifford Pinchot, the leading exponent of the "wise use" school. Thereafter Muir poured all his energies into the cause of preservation, particularly the national park movement. Yet Pinchot, WJ McGee, Frederick H. Newell, Francis G. Newlands, and James R. Garfield among others were directing federal resource policy toward utilitarianism and even succeeded in appropriating the term "conservation" for their viewpoint. The Pinchot-dominated governors' conference on the conservation of natural resources held at the White House in 1908 revealed the depth of the schism. Spokesmen for the protection and preservation of nature, including John Muir, were kept off the guest lists in favor of practical men who interpreted conservation to mean the maintenance of an abundance of important raw materials. The frustrated advocates of wilderness preservation had no choice but to call Pinchot a "deconservationist."

Meanwhile William Kent was construing conservation in his own way. For him the central issue was the future of republicanism. If private interests took precedence over the people's voice in regard to natural resources, democracy was endangered as well as the land. Kent became concerned about this possibility in 1909 and campaigned vigorously against what he conceived to be the attempt of the Truckee River Power Company to obtain rights to Lake Tahoe detrimental to the public interest. The following year the controversy over a private company's rights to Alaskan coal lands brought Kent to Pinchot's side in opposition to Secretary of the Interior Richard A. Ballinger. In Kent's mind it was the archetype Progressive cause with "predatory interests"

standing against "the birthright of Americans." Indeed, he conceived of conservation as the people's best weapon against concentrated wealth. If the conservationists and the democratic impulse they expressed did not prevail, Kent believed "there is nothing ahead of us but a trend toward peonage." Understandably, Kent could encourage Pinchot in January, 1910, that his battle with Ballinger was "a crisis in the history of the country which, if settled one way, will lead to progress along democratic lines, and if settled the other way will be a harbinger of revolution." In this frame of mind Kent welcomed the idea of *public* control of natural resources as a panacea for land policy as well as for American government. And most importantly for his relationship to Muir, Kent's conception of conservation accorded greater value to democratic development of natural resources than to wilderness preservation.

Shortly after the Ballinger-Pinchot dispute, the Hetch Hetchy controversy moved into the conservation spotlight, deepening the rift in conservation ranks and bringing the friendship of John Muir and William Kent to an abrupt end. Situated on a dry, sandy peninsula, the city of San Francisco faced a chronic fresh-water shortage. In the Sierra, about one hundred and fifty miles distant, the erosive action of glaciers and the Tuolumne River had scooped the spectacular, high-walled Hetch Hetchy Valley. Engineers had long recognized its suitability as a reservoir and source of hydro-electric power, but in 1890 the act creating Yosemite National Park designated the valley and its environs a wilderness preserve. Undaunted, San Francisco applied for Hetch Hetchy shortly after the turn of the century, and, riding a wave of public sympathy generated by the disastrous earthquake of 1906, obtained preliminary federal approval of its plans.

John Muir, however, determined to arouse a nation-wide protest over what he conceived to be a needless sacrifice of wilderness values and a betrayal of the whole idea of national parks. In the five years after 1908, while the Hetch Hetchy question was before Congress, Muir labored to convince his countrymen that wild parks were essential, "for everybody needs beauty as well as bread, places to play in and pray in where Nature may heal and cheer and give strength to body and soul alike." As such a statement implied, nature, for Muir, was steeped in spiritual truth. Its desecration for material reasons was sacrilege. He had no doubt that he was doing the Lord's battle in resisting the reservoir. San Francisco became "the Prince of the powers of Darkness" and "Satan and Co." This conviction that he was engaged in a battle between right and wrong prompted Muir and his school of conservationists to issue vituperative outbursts against the opposition. In a popular book of 1912 Muir labeled them "temple destroyers" who scorned the "God of the Mountains" in pursuit of the "Almighty Dollar." Using such arguments, and playing upon the growing American enthusiasm for wildness in both man and nature, Muir succeeded in stimulating a remarkable amount of public concern for Hetch Hetchy.

As a California congressman and well-known conservationist, William Kent could not ignore the Hetch Hetchy question. On March 31, 1911, a few weeks after he arrived in Washington to begin his first term, Kent received a personal letter from John Muir. Assuming that Kent, the donor of Muir Woods, would champion the cause of wilderness preservation, Muir simply encouraged him to watch

developments concerning Hetch Hetchy closely and "do lots of good work." But for Kent the matter was not so simple. He realized Hetch Hetchy was an extraordinary wilderness area and part of a national park. But he also knew that the powerful Pacific Gas and Electric Company wanted Hetch Hetchy as a step toward tightening its hold on California hydro-electric resources. Municipal control of Hetch Hetchy's water would block this plan and at the same time be a significant victory for the ideal of public ownership. The sacrifice of wilderness qualities, Kent concluded, was regrettable but in this case necessary for a greater good. Making this point in a letter to Muir's colleague, Robert Underwood Johnson, Kent stated his conviction that conservation could best be served by granting the valley to San Francisco.

In 1913 the Hetch Hetchy struggle entered its climactic phase, and as a second-term congressman and key member of the house committee on the public lands, Kent was in a position to exert considerable influence. He began by helping draft a bill granting the valley to San Francisco and insuring that the resulting electricity would be publicly controlled; then he opened his home to the city's supporters as a campaign headquarters. The fact that Kent was known as the donor of Muir Woods lent extra weight to his opinions. Certainly *he* would not dismiss the claims of wilderness preservation lightly. Kent exploited this advantage fully. When the Hetch Hetchy bill was under consideration in the house, he rose to answer the preservationists' arguments: "I can lay claim to being a nature lover myself. I think that is a matter of record." He then proceeded to defend the reservoir plans as "the highest and best type of conservation." The same technique appeared in a letter to President Woodrow Wilson where Kent asserted that in the cause of protecting nature he had "spent more time and effort . . . than any of the men who are opposing this bill." And there was, in fact, much truth in this claim.

The final stages of the Hetch Hetchy controversy revealed just how far apart Muir and Kent had drawn. "Dam Hetch Hetchy!" cried Muir, "as well dam for water-tanks the people's cathedrals and churches, for no holier temple has ever been consecrated by the heart of man." Mustering the Sierra Club and wilderness advocates throughout the country, the elderly Californian threw his remaining energy into what he regarded as the most crucial conservation struggle of his life-time. Kent's emphasis, on the other hand, was all on the beneficence of public ownership. Speaking in the house, he declared that "the ideal conservation is public social use of resources of our country without waste." Non-use, Kent explained, which the preservation of wilderness entailed, was waste. Searching for a dramatic illustration, he declared it his sentiment that if Niagara Falls could be totally used up in providing for humanity's need for water, he would be "glad to sacrifice that scenic wonder." According to Kent, "all things are relative," and the benefits of having a wild Hetch Hetchy must yield to the greater advantages involved in producing hydro-power and creating a water supply "upon which not a cent of private profit shall ever be made." He had made up his mind that "real conservation meant proper use and not locking up of natural resources" and the furtherance of democracy through their public development.

It remained for Kent, as an acknowledged admirer of Muir to provide public explanation for their divergence over Hetch Hetchy. He did so in the summer of 1913 in a series of letters to his congressional colleagues. To Representative Sydney Anderson of Minnesota he wrote:

I hope you will not take my friend, Muir, seriously, for he is a man entirely without social sense. With him, it is me and God and the rock where God put it, and that is the end of the story. I know him well and as far as this proposition is concerned, he is mistaken.

Similarly he wired Pinchot that the Hetch Hetchy protest was the work of private power interests using "misinformed nature lovers" as their spokesmen. In October Kent told a public gathering in California that because Muir had spent so much time in the wilderness he had not acquired the social instincts of the average man.

The nearest Kent came to accounting directly to Muir was an undated memorandum to the Society for the Preservation of National Parks, of which Muir was a director. After commending the group for its statement on Hetch Hetchy, Kent reiterated his conviction that the "highest form of conservation" called for a reservoir that would provide Californians with an abundant supply of cheap water. "I make these comments," Kent concluded, "with the utmost regard for your sincerity of purpose, and with a full understanding of your point of view."

Muir never responded directly to these remarks, but in the year of his life that remained after the reservoir plan received federal approval in December, 1913, he must have felt betrayed. The man who had done him his greatest honor in creating Muir Woods became an influential opponent in the Hetch Hetchy fight. But it was not that Kent changed his mind about wilderness after 1908. At the very time he was helping draft the bill authorizing a reservoir in Hetch Hetchy, he asked Gifford Pinchot for a statement in support of a state park on Mount Tamalpais. Specifically, Kent wanted Pinchot to show "the advantage of such a wilderness, particularly near San Francisco." And after Hetch Hetchy, Kent went on to author the bill establishing the National Park Service (1916), participate in the founding of the Save-the-Redwoods League (1918), and add more land to Muir Woods National Monument (1920). At his memorial service in 1928 one of the chief speakers was William E. Colby, president of the Sierra Club. Kent's problem was that the necessity to decide about Hetch Hetchy left no room for an expression of his ambivalence. The valley could not simultaneously be a wilderness and a publicly owned, power-producing reservoir.

In spite of their common interest in wilderness, Kent and Muir ultimately gave it a different priority. The result was a bitter conflict. Yet both men were sincere and energetic proponents of conservation. Indeed, few Americans after their generation openly opposed it. But that hardly ended the controversy over the value and uses of nature in America. One man's conservation was frequently another's exploitation, which is another way of saying that conservationists neither were nor are a homogeneous interest group or political bloc. As the relationship of Kent and Muir revealed, the dynamics of the history of the American landscape in the twentieth century comes not so much from "conservationists" embattled against greedy, wasteful exploiters, but from the conflict of diverse interpretations of the meaning of conserving natural resources.

Some scholars, like FRANK G. SPECK (1881–1950), contend that the American Indians were good stewards of their environment. Others argue that only the lack of technology prevented greater exploitation. But the Indians' social thought and religion contained the seeds of ideas that subsequently formed the basis of the ecological perspective. Even with a power saw in his hand there is reason to suspect that the pre-Columbian Indian would have been environmentally responsible. Among recent environmentalists, at any rate, the Indian and his way of life command increasing admiration. Speck was an anthropologist with a particular interest in the relation of the American Indians to the land.

Frank G. Speck

Indians as Ecologists

Do uncivilized tibes know the virtues of conservation? The question would seem to require an answer in the negative in view of what is generally believed to represent the intelligence standard of peoples who have not reached the status of advanced civilization. Surprising though it may seem, the answer is, nevertheless, in the affirmative so far as the tribes of the eastern and northern forests of the continent are concerned. Contrary to the prevailing idea as respects native ownership of the land, the Algonkian Indians, from the Atlantic to the Great Lakes, carried on their hunting in restricted, family hunting territories descending from generation to generation in the male line. It was in these family tracts that the supply of game animals was maintained by deliberate systems of rotation in hunting and gathering, and defended by the family groups as a heritage from some remote time when the country had been given to their ancestors by the Creator. Before glancing at some details of the principles operating in the protection of native wild life from extermination by over-hunting, let us consider what an eminent student of law has said regarding the nature of property itself.

"For purposes of social theory property is to be conceived in terms of the control of man over things. Man needs food to eat, implements to procure it, land to work upon . . . That he may supply his needs at all he must at least temporarily control . . . the spot on which he

From Frank G. Speck, "Aboriginal Conservators," *Audubon Magazine* (1938), pp. 258–261.

is working. But that this temporary control or possession may become property, certain further conditions are essential. His possession must in the first place be recognized by others, *i.e.,* it must be of the nature of a right . . . With regard to things of a permanent nature his right must also have a certain permanence. He must be able to count on the use of the thing. His right . . . must be respected in his absence. Thirdly, his control must be exclusive." Hence, the tenure of land among the Indians of the Atlantic forests and eastern Canada conforms to something like "naked possession"—the maintenance of a supply of animal and vegetable life, methods of insuring its propagation to provide sources of life for posterity, the permanent family residence within well-known and oftentimes blazed property boundaries, and resentment against trespass by the family groups surrounding them who possessed districts of their own. And withal, the remarkably complete knowledge of breeding habits, the food and protective requirements of animals in the territory, are striking features of the "science" which these aborigines applied to the conservation of their resources. The student of primitive institutions finds in various parts of the world similar regulations invented and practiced for the same purposes, nearly always in regions where mankind lived in a purely hunting stage of culture and whose other characteristics were so simple, possibly even initial, as to entitle them to classification as "savages." This remark applies to the primitive hunting peoples of northeastern Asia, Australia, parts of the Pacific, extreme South Africa, and Fuegia. It would seem that in the early stages of human cultural growth we have evidence of an understanding of the need of sustaining the balance of nature. Those tribes of mankind with limited material equipment had achieved a balance with nature which the more advanced "civilized" groups have lost, with their phenomenal increase of material equipment.

Let us, however, glance at the conditions of wild-life conservation as we discover them among the Indians with whom the present paper proposes to treat. . . . I might summarize the circumstances as follows: "economically these territories were regulated in a wise and interesting manner. The game was kept account of very closely, so that the proprietors knew about how abundant each kind of animal was, and hence could regulate the killing so as not to deplete the stock." The hunting and gathering which furnished the food supply of these people was by no means a hit-or-miss random search. Their dependence upon limited resources in limited territories required provision for themselves and their descendants, and they took stock of their resources. They knew in some detail what the supply of each resource was: deer, moose, beaver, fur-bearers, edible birds, berries, roots, trees, wild grasses. They knew the districts where each was to be found when wanted and, roughly, in what quantities. These remarks demonstrate the lines of aboriginal thought in the direction of economic conservation in a manner not unlike what administrators conceive to be the necessary means for preserving the balance of nature in behalf of protection against the depletion of game supply, forest cover, vegetable resources and water-shed safeguarding.

Aside from these material considerations, we are forced to realize the existence of aesthetic appreciation of the meaning of nature at large among Indians in the hunting level. The native attitude toward wild life, both plant and animal in all forms, is one which takes stock of religious associations, even governing the lives of individuals and groups. Various families and clans among these people held themselves in special relationships to groups of animals, associations which have earned the name of "totemism." It would be futile here to discuss what arguments this term has provoked among sociologists, but we may admit that among these tribes no individual could feel himself to be free from certain obligations owed to particular animals, oftentimes to less active forms of life such as trees and plants. The animal world, in their view, enjoyed the right to exist in close association with human beings. Through the coöperation of human, animal, and plant life, the will of the supreme being, the Creator, was carried out. This teaching permitted no wasteful or arbitrary destruction of life in any form. In taking animals for food or for skin, the survivors, as breeding resources, were constantly considered, and the life thus taken was atoned for by rituals of address, apologizing in sympathetic phrases for their death. They were thanked for the sacrifice they made to man and death-rites were performed for them with rituals of thanksgiving. Similar rulings were applied to the gathering of plant life and trees when taken for medicine, firewood or bark. The recording, presentation and study of these abundant rituals is the task of ethnologists now working among the various tribes. Even plants when gathered for food or medicine were approached with reverence and pulled up with discretion through consideration of their own welfare, not only man's. To tear up plants by the roots in quantities is to the Eastern aborigines like massacre; to separate two pipsissewa plants growing near each other is, for instance, like disrupting the family [unit of a] small and friendly circle by the slaying of parent or child. I have even heard that when one such plant is removed, the other is discovered wilted and dead the next day, or the survivor may have moved off to join another mate. Numerous regulations govern the taking and killing of plant and animal life. With these people no act of this sort is profane, hunting is not war upon the animals, not a slaughter for food or profit, but a *holy occupation*.

All in all, such refinements in attitudes toward nature may seem amazing to civilized man whose point of view toward natural life in all forms has departed so far from a state of harmony with its existence. The liberal naturalist of today would find himself in thorough accord with such "savages," who see in the world about them the coöperating forces which make life smooth and full. It did not require a Thoreau of less than a century ago to reawaken the sense of nature appreciation in the minds of Eastern Indians. Ages of harmonious co-living with the life of the forests, swamps and ravines of the eastern woodland, left them the sense to accord to all forms of life the right to live, to propagate and fulfill their own destinies, as man himself claims it. This assertion is made with no degree of exaggeration. It is rather understated, for to treat its evidence will require volumes on ethnology, some of which are now in course of preparation. One could separate the materialistic purposes of conservation among the Eastern and Northern Indians from spiritual and imaginative aspects of communion with life and discover the predominance of the latter in native thought on nature. Noyes, Kilmer, and Isaiah would find their poetical creations, which visualize trees as sentient beings, exceeded by "savage" poets in the northern forests, who sing of the Creator as "combing the hair of his children as would a father, when the trees are seen bending beneath the force of the wind," of the vegetation on earth being "hair on the body of mother earth who gives them their life," of the trees "praying to the Creator in their own tongue when the wind causes the leaves to sigh and rustle." Such phrases bring to mind the Old Testament animations in describing trees as clapping their hands with joy, as letting "the sea roar and the fields be joyful, then shall all the trees of the woods rejoice before the Lord." And we may not forget Kilmer's reference to the tree that "lifts her leafy arms to pray." And again Noyes: "In the weary cry of the wind and the whisper of flower and tree."

So why do we think of ourselves as teachers of a higher order of nature-aesthetics in a newer, but historically merely a rediscovered, attitude toward life of the wild, and Nature in her totality, as being a solace, an entity with a soul, perhaps a God? We may be loath to admit that economic interests dominate the European attitude toward creations on earth, but our anxiety over questions of wealth still rules our minds and decisions. The classical epos, "Man is one world and has another to attend him," means one thing to the economic conservator and another to the pure naturalist and his brother-in-creed, the aborigine of the eastern forests.

Man-against-nature is a familiar idea in our culture. Yet once, presumably, man was a part of nature. Civilization did not exist. There was no distinction between "indoors" and "outdoors." CLARENCE J. GLACKEN (b. 1909) is an historical geographer interested in how western man diverged from his original posture through the series of environmental transformations we call civilization. His essay throws considerable light on both the nature of and the resistance to the ecological perspective. Glacken's *Traces on the Rhodian Shore: Nature and Culture in Western Thought From Ancient Times to the End of the Eighteenth Century* is a monumental study of ancient attitudes and behavior respecting the environment.

Clarence J. Glacken

Man Versus *Nature?*

Outmoded means out of fashion or obsolete, no longer able to fulfill a proper function. I am not certain, therefore, that the title of this discussion is a precise one. For outmoded does not mean tired or lacking in energy or virility. The world is full of outmoded ideas which are still very strong and give no indication of dying off. . . .

"Man against nature." "Man's mastery over nature." These dichotomies are often thought to be the only important concepts in Western civilization expressing the relationship between the two. Frequently, the "Western" concept of dominance or opposition has been contrasted with "Eastern" concepts of harmony and union with nature, but I believe this contrast oversimplifies matters. Like all other great civilizations, Western civilization is not monolithic in its summations, and it has nourished all sorts of different ideas. There is no question, however, that the man-nature dichotomy has been and continues to be extremely important and, although challenged, it has held its own in popular thought and has, in addition, diffused to many parts of the non-Western world.

I have the impression, however, that the concept of man against nature is not typical of the history of thought as a whole, or of the ideas of prehistoric and so-called primitive peoples. And even if one has reservations about applying the I-Thou, I-It concepts of Martin Buber, as some have done, to the relation of prehistoric and primitive man to nature. I think it comes closer to the mark to say that these peoples thought of themselves more as identified with rather than pitted against nature. . . . In contrast to modern man, prehistoric peoples enjoyed a close, lively association and identification with nature—as if it were a "thou" instead of an "it." This is an interesting approach, but we still know too little about the matter to make distinctions. The area is still poorly explored, but the evidence seems to indicate a widespread feeling of closeness of human to other kinds of life. . . . This probability is reinforced by recent ethnographic studies which emphasize the intimate knowledge that primitive peoples have of their environment.

The idea of man against nature is thus, in my opinion, more parochial than universal. Admittedly it has achieved great strength in Western thought, but we must recognize that it is parochial because, despite powerful influences toward uniformity of ideas through mass media, other non-Western cultures, with their own values, still exist. The recognition of such parochialism forces us to ask why and under what circumstances the idea of man against nature grew up and has prospered until this day.

One reason for the lasting strength of the idea has been that in modern times it became, in variant forms, the basis for a secular philosophy of history. In this philosophy the course of civilization was seen as a movement, an evolution from a time in which man was under the control of nature to a point at which the situation is reversed and man is in control of nature. The interpretation is closely tied up with the desire to ameliorate the human condition by cultivating the arts and sciences, an idea which gradually developed in the eighteenth and nineteenth centuries into the idea of progress, progress often but not always being seen in terms of both a divorcement from nature and a mastery over it. A primordial harmony was assumed before the coming of man, but man in his progress would gradually humanize the world, creating through technological inventions an even more exalted harmony through his struggles and labors.

I would distinguish between two traditions of the idea of man against nature in Western thought, the first being derived from the Old Testament, especially Genesis 1; the second, a product of modern times, for which I would cite the philosophy of Francis Bacon as a convenient marker without insisting that it is the actual place and time of origin.

The lines of Genesis are indeed striking. In Genesis 1: 20-28 a distinction is made between the acts of God with relationship to all life except man and the acts of God with relationship to man. In the one case, all life is to increase and to multiply; in the other, man is not only to do the same, but also to "have dominion over the fish of the sea and over the birds of the air and over every living thing that moves upon the earth." This is reaffirmed by God after the flood and a new start for the human race with Noah, his three sons, and their wives.

These Genesis verses have taken on a new and ironical meaning in recent decades and in the immediate present because much has been learned in the last century about culture and environment, especially the effects of the former on the latter. The acts of man ranging from deforestation to air pollution and nuclear warfare and the multiplication of man have given dramatic proof of his obedience to the orders of God for all life to multiply and for human life, in addition to multiplying, to have dominion over the rest of the creation. . . .

One of the most famous apothegms of Bacon was that we cannot command nature except by obeying her, and perhaps here we should think of "obeying" as implying "knowing" also. There are many pertinent illustrations but I will confine myself to *The New Atlantis,* in which one sees a philosopher ambitious to reject the scholastic philosophy as a teaching of inactivity, to promote the arts and the sciences, encouraging invention in order to change nature and to adapt it for human uses. In *The New Atlantis,* Bacon compares the great voyages of discovery which have opened the horizons of man with the continued narrowness of man's intellectual vision. Thus, it is essentially a program for the control of nature by man, a creative broadening act comparable in spirit to what he saw in the voyages of discovery. . . .

If this admittedly incomplete analysis is correct, the early modern form of the contrast between man and nature was viewed less in terms of struggle, more in terms of creativity, and for two reasons:

1. The struggle with and the control over nature were ways of depicting the progress of civilization. In its material aspects, civilization meant this—the purposive changes in nature, the overcoming of natural obstacles by bridges, drainage, roads, and later by railroads and air and sea routes.

2. There was little awareness or study of the age-old cumulative but unnoticed effects of man's activities in changing the environment. There is ample evidence of local awareness but such knowledge was not widely diffused. Lacking is that crescendo of complaint, based on ecological theory, about destruction of the environment by man so characteristic of the last 100 years and now so common that it appears in articles in *Science* magazine, in Sunday supplements, and in presidential addresses.

By the nineteenth century some glaring inadequacies of this idea were apparent; they are still. We can regard one phase of the romantic movement, despite its complexity, as a rebellion against the dichotomy between man and nature. In the movement for the protection of nature, we owe much to romantic ideas of the beauties of untouched and remote wildernesses, and of the importance of being conscious of our attitudes to the natural world.

In the nineteenth century, the idea of man's control over nature or man against nature was closely linked with the idea of indefinite and inevitable progress. Even today its vitality, I think, is owing to its association with vague, popular, poorly examined notions of progress, even if this progress has no more meaning than that a statistic of the current year in some desirable category is greater than it was for the previous year. Technology and invention were grist to this mill because they represented clear and easily verified successes. . . . The optimism was based on material progress, on the idea that this high rational civilization in its onward motion not only advanced itself but was producing humanized environments which went along with it. It is true that especially toward the end of the century a literature questioning technology and its effects began to take form but, on the whole one sees in Western civilization of the nineteenth century the apogee of faith in science and technology—under the rubric of "control over nature."

In the second half of the century, however, the seeds of alternate views were planted. . . . The concept revealed short-comings as a unifier of a body of ideas and its concomitant knowledge. These short-comings have in the main survived to the present. What are they? First, the concept is narrow and restrictive—and subject to the same criticism of the conception of man in the earlier traditional concepts of design and teleology. To say of the earth that it has been designed by a Creator for the sake of all life is one thing; to say that it is made for man alone and to use as he sees fit is another. The anthropo-centrism of the latter is narrow and crippling. In the secular versions, which follow, the narrow and crippling anthro-pocentrism continues in the assumption of universal utility for man. All nature be-comes a resource.

Furthermore, the emphasis was on the dichotomy, on two worlds, the world of man and the world of nature. I believe also that the dichotomy encouraged the study of man within the framework of human institutions alone, his struggle with and his control over nature, being activities carried on within the purview of these human institutions. It tended to discourage an organic view; beauty, vari-ety, plentitude could be celebrated in art, music, literature. It encouraged a utili-tarian view of nature, not a preserving or conserving one: the former was pro-gressive, the latter romantic, an incurable clinging to the past. But its most mis-leading aspect, especially when it was an indistinguishable element of the idea of progress, was the high plane on which it placed man and his institutions. He dominated nature by rationality and purpose.

Too much rationality was assumed in the changes that brought about this con-trol over nature, this progress. Mastery was the mastery of intelligence and plan-ning. One feels in reading the optimistic literature of the period that the rational-ity of civilization was taken for granted. The belief was widespread that a great gulf separated primitive peoples and the peoples of European cultures. We now know—it was known then too by many—that the assumption of rationality in civi-lization is very misleading. Today there is too much evidence to the contrary—so overwhelming that it requires little dis-cussion. The assumption of rationality, that Western civilization was at the apex of civilizations in the march of progress, implied that mastery was rational mas-tery, that masters of nature were rational masters. . . .

In the . . . argument over evolution and special creation . . . is . . . the case for examining the interrelationships in na-ture. These were seen on the model of a web of life. The fact that such interrela-tions exist in the organic world did not have to await [Charles] Darwin's expo-sition,* they were part of the design argument, and at the basis of eighteenth-century observations in natural history. God in his wisdom had made the earth and all the living matter in it as a part of an overall rational design, and it was to be expected that everything would fit, that there would be intricate interrela-tionships in the natural world, replete with adaptations.

But Darwin saw balances and har-monies in nature, webs of life—today we call them ecosystems—as the result of evolutionary processes, products of time, circumstance, selection. This restatement of the concept of a unity and harmony of nature provided the basis for the building of modern ecological theory. In the cats-to-clover chain, the number of cats is related indirectly to the number of mice, bees, and clover, but it is also related to old maids, and the growth of

---

*Darwin published *The Origin of Species* in 1859. –Ed.

Scotch fir is related to man's grazing animals and the building of fences. A fresh opportunity was created for reconsidering the question of man's place in nature—not vertically as was so popular at the time in the sense of his place in a hierarchy of being . . . but horizontally, his activities as part of the organic world as well as of an economic, social, or political world. . . .

[George Perkins] Marsh also used the idea of a balance or harmony of nature, not in the way that Darwin applied it (as a general concept bearing on a theory of evolution) but as a measuring device for gauging the force of human agency in modifying the environment. He was concerned with historical questions: the effects of domestication, deforestation, and the control of water and sand dunes. Many of the effects of human interference with the environment were unsuspected, and the vistas thus opened were far broader and deeper than the narrower confines of the idea of purposive control over nature.

Implicit in Marsh's work* is the idea that earth history since the coming of man could be written in part as the history of cumulative change by human agency. . . . Human history, observed Marsh, may be the history of man's gradual divorcement from nature; but it is also the history of displacements in the organic world, of the habitats of plants, animals and primitive peoples. Domestic plants and especially animals became extensions of human agency, of human will. The result was to suggest the poverty of history written within the human framework alone, the poverty of interpreting such changes as chapters in economic history. The great theme was that the cumulative force of human

Man and Nature; or, Physical Geography as Modified by Human Action was published in 1864.—Ed.

agency could be irreversible, could bring about such deterioration that the planet could become uninhabitable. . . .

The web of life by Darwin provided new opportunities for interpretations of the significance of the idea of balances and harmonies; it was the latest attempt to find a construct for the study of the natural world. Marsh made vivid and clear the strong interconnections between the nature of man and human culture and the environment; he showed that civilization inevitably has not created and will not create new and rational harmonies in the natural environment. . . .

Thus, a gradually developing body of thought which recognizes that civilization might be progressing or at least changing while the environment might be deteriorating obviously confronts man with a new set of circumstances. Modern pessimism, alarm, and dissatisfaction with the concept of man against nature accompany a loss of faith in progress that has become widespread in this century. Too often civilization means a destruction and chaos of nature, not a softening and a rationalization of it. Today we do not need ideas or philosophies to tell us this. None of us would automatically embrace a declaration that environments become more beautiful as civilizations advance. Our eyes, our ears, and our noses tell us quite the contrary. . . .

The concept of man against nature as a philosophy has lost whatever creative force it had in the past. Over the last 100 years the ideas of ecological interrelationships, of the web of life put forward by Darwin . . . and of the contemporary ecosystem concept have been growing to challenge the traditional dichotomies such as man and nature, man versus nature, man against nature, man's control over nature, or progress as a divorcement from nature.

WILBUR R. JACOBS (b. 1918) who specializes in the history of the American West and the American Indian, here points an accusing finger at his fellow historians for failing to call a spade a spade. Compare Jacobs' account to that in any American history textbook with which you are familiar. Do you see how radical he is in his revisionist stance? What do you think of historians like Jacobs who step out of the "ivory tower" of allegedly objective scholarship and use history as a tool for reform?

Wilbur R. Jacobs

Revising History with Ecology

We read in recent news reports that our fish and wildlife are being slaughtered by the thousands. Conservationists warn us that many types of birds and animals are in danger of extinction here and abroad as expanding human population relentlessly squeezes them out of wilderness sanctuaries. Even breathing is difficult in air dangerously polluted by millions of automobiles and a huge industrial complex. Many of our lakes and rivers are contaminated, and even our beaches are blacked by sludge washed in from the sea.

The destruction of our natural environment is usually viewed as a great modern problem, the implication being that only in the twentieth century has the onslaught taken place. There is growing realization, however, that from the beginning of our history we Americans have been both destructive and wasteful of natural resources. It is actually the scale of the damage instead of its newness which forces us, though still reluctantly, to confront the problem today.

We historians must bear some responsibility for the lateness of our awakening, for we really have not done our homework. We have avoided and in most cases ignored the complicated series of historical phenomena that brought about our dilemma. Our histories, particularly our frontier-sectional or "western" histories,

Reprinted by permission of the American Historical Association. Wilbur R. Jacobs, "Frontiersmen, Fur Traders, and Other Varmints, An Ecological Appraisal of the Frontier in American History," *American Historical Association Newsletter* (November, 1970), pp. 5–11.

tend to give us a glowing get-rich-quick chronicle of the conquest of the continent. As Frederick Jackson Turner wrote in his influential essay of 1893, ". . . the Indian trade pioneered the way for civilization . . . the trails widened into roads, and the roads into turnpikes, and these in turn were transformed into railroads. . . . In this progress from savage conditions lie topics for the evolutionist." The Turnerean theme of "progress' of American civilization has generally reflected itself in American social attitudes toward the wilderness. The Indian is viewed as a "consolidating influence" on frontiersmen who banded together for defense. When the tribesman is brought into the story, he is depicted as a kind of obstacle to the westward movement. The Indian's respect for animal life and reverence for the land, when mentioned, are usually dismissed as superstition. Unlike the Indian, the white man, with a Judeo-Christian ethic stressing man's dominance over nature, had no religious scruples about exploiting the wilderness. From the beginning, fur traders, who had rum to encourage warriors to hunt, were often frustrated by the reluctance of natives to busy themselves in the useful activity of scouring the woods for furs and skins. Modern American social attitudes toward wild animals show a persistence of the fur trader's point of view. Unless a species can be fitted into a category of being particularly "useful" in a commercial sense, there is public apathy about its survival. A good illustration is public acceptance of an extensive government poisoning project designed to exterminate coyotes in several western states, but so indiscriminately and carelessly administered that serious damage is being done to so-called "non-target species" as well.

This strictly utilitarian attitude toward wilderness life, though widespread in American society, has been partially balanced by a countertheme of appreciation of the wilderness by such writers as Francis Parkman, Henry David Thoreau, John Muir, and Aldo Leopold. They identified wild country and wild animals with genuine human freedom. If we have no free-roaming wild life in wild country, they argued, then we eliminate space for that remaining wild thing, the irrepressible human spirit.

Do historians have an obligation to help counteract harmful social attitudes about the environment that run contrary to the best interests of the nation at large? It is a question that has plagued the consciences of some of our best writers, including Francis Parkman and Frederick Jackson Turner. Certainly we historians have no responsibility for what has happened in the past, but we do have access to historic records and knowledge of what earlier generations did or failed to do. The public and students can expect, therefore, that we will make available the fruits of our investigations in a form undistorted by patriotism, prejudice, sentiment, ignorance, or lopsided research. But such a presentation of the American past is, in certain areas of history, not always the rule. This criticism can be applied particularly to specific subjects in "frontier" or "westward movement" history.

Historians of the American frontier, for instance, have failed to impress their readers with the utterly destructive impact that the fur trade had upon the North American continent and the American Indian. There are no investigations of the role the fur men had in killing off certain types of wildlife, which in turn had a permanent effect upon the land and upon native and white societies. The traders and their followers, the fur trading companies, are usually depicted as positive benefactors in the development of American civilization as it moved westward from the Appalachians to the Pacific Coast. Indeed, the story of the fur trade is almost always (and perhaps unconsciously) told with a capitalistic bias. The historian usually expresses a businessman's outlook in describing the development and expansion of this mercantile enterprise. If the fur trade contributed to the rapid economic growth of the country, and it unquestionably did (Walter Prescott Webb argued that it helped to develop a boom economy in the first two centuries of our history), then the implication is the fur trade was a good thing for all Americans. Free furs and skins, free land, free minerals; it was all part of the great westward trek and "The Development of American Society," according to F. J. Turner and his followers. The self-made man, the heroic figure, who conquered the wilderness was the free trapper, the mountain man. Because the history of trading does not naturally attract the reader's interest, historians of the frontier have often gilded their flawed lily with a bit of spurious romanticism. The bear and bison hunter becomes the courageous tamer of the wilderness.

The real question of interpretation here is: who is the real varmint, the bear or the trapper who killed him? Aside from the fact that bears are sometimes noted for anti-social behavior, our frontier historians have not had a problem in answering such a question because their interpretations have been conditioned by a society steeped in a *laissez-faire* business ideology. Our view of progress — one which permeates all groups of society and leads us to accept without question the need for an expanding economy — is that progress consists in exploitation and growth, which in turn depends on com-

mercialization and the conquest of nature. In our histories we have treated the land more as a commodity than as a resource. We have here in a nutshell the conquistador mentality that has so long dominated the writing of much American history.

Until recently historians have largely ignored the ecological challenge. Yet truthful, interesting American history, double-barreled and difficult to write, is in part the revolting story of how we managed to commercialize all that we could harness and control with our technical skills. It is, in its unvarnished state, an unpleasant narrative of the reckless exploitation of minerals, waterways, soil, timber, wildlife, wilderness, and Indians, a part of a larger story of man's rape of nature over centuries. Can historians ignore the fact that today we can no longer afford such cruelty and wastefulness? Do we have an obligation to help our fellow-Americans in learning the art of frugality in husbanding our resources? If we as historians hope to foster an awareness of the dangers of further greedy exploitation of the land, we must examine our history in detail to see what has led up to our present situation.

The earliest exploiters of the American continent, the first to tamper seriously with the ecological balance that had existed for centuries relatively undisturbed by aboriginal tribes (such as the Iroquois who depended upon an economy closely governed by the ecology of the northeastern forest), were the colonial traders and trappers. Their successors, the American trapper-frontiersmen, have been blown up into heroes in our histories. Turner in his 1893 essay helped to shape the myth. His enthusiasm for pioneer types proved to be so infectious that we have tended to accept his interpretations, ignoring the fact that men of the trapper-trader fraternity were often unscrupulous, lawless, and hungry for personal gain. These rascals and pleasure-hunters destroyed without scruple countless beavers, otters, large and small carnivores, and the great bison herds that once lived on our grasslands and woodlands. Even Turner in later years reached the conclusion that pioneers were "wasteful and seeking quick results rather than conservation and permanence."

Can we stand back as historians and look at the American western migration as a huge page in social history to see how clearly the story of the frontier advance is also the story of the looting and misuse of the land? The traders who led the procession of pioneers through the Cumberland Gap and the South Pass were the vanguard of those who slaughtered beaver, buffalo, and antelope and thus reduced the western Indian tribes to a state of semi-starvation, making them easy victims for sporadic white military campaigns. Ironically the individual fur traders, miners, and cattle raisers were, in many cases, ruined by powerful combines devoted to large-scale commercialization of the natural resources of the West. Because of our exaggerated respect for the entrepreneur (or the pioneer or frontiersman, as we have often called him), we as historians have failed to condemn this early rape of the land, just as today—and for the same reasons—we have not joined visibly in the condemnation of industrial pollution.

How can historians assess the damage brought about by allowing commercial interests to override our best national interests? We might begin by an attempt to gauge the effects of the substitution within a half century of hundreds of thousands of horses and domestic cattle for wild hoofed animals that existed in the huge area of the Louisiana Purchase. What effect did this have on the fertility of the land and the balance of nature? Can we as historians join scientists in calling attention to the important principle that the earth's productivity depends upon an organic cycle, an order of nature in which organic material taken from the earth must be returned to it? The violation of this principle by Americans in the eighteenth and nineteenth centuries was responsible for the destruction of a great virgin wilderness. In this destruction the substitution of annual grasses for the life-sustaining primordial prairie sod of middle America is one of the more momentous happenings in American history, but the subject is something less than a favorite with historians of the frontier.

Those who hope to write about significant historic events of this kind (and consequences arising out of them) will need a sort of knowledge not ordinarily possessed by historians. To study the impact the fur trade had upon America, for instance, we must have more than a beginning acquaintance with ethnology, botany, silviculture, biology, zoology, and indeed much of the physical sciences. Our doctoral programs for budding American historians are in drastic need of revision if we hope to train qualified candidates who can write intelligently about the history of the exploitation of the land. In addition, there is a sophisticated body of thought about the value of wilderness to Americans that should be studied. There is often difference between what wilderness is and what we *think* it is. Francis Parkman, perhaps our greatest historian, trained himself to write about the Indian, the American forest, and early American civilization. At one time a professor of horticulture, he understood and loved the American forest; he understood, therefore, the respect for nature among the Indians. He is a rare example of a historian who took the trouble to educate himself so that he could "manage," as he said, "to tell things as they really happened."

But the writers who followed Parkman did not follow his methods or his example. Those historians who dominated later frontier historical writing were in many respects prejudiced against the land, the wilderness, and the animal life in it. The historiography of the fur trade is a kind of case study of the larger problem of rewriting the history of the American frontier. The old guard of the fur trade history—Hiram M. Chittenden, Harold A. Innis, Douglas MacKay, Reuben Gold Thwaites, Wayne E. Stevens, Frederick Jackson Turner (and some of his pupils and disciples, especially Louise P. Kellogg, Albert Volwiler, and Robert Glass Cleland)—have left us with a one-sided view of the fur trade in American history. Though Chittenden, Turner, and Cleland loved the wilderness and spoke against the despoliation of nature, all bear a responsibility for the romanticizing of the traders. Cleland's approach to the mountain trappers as a "reckless breed of men" conferred on them a spurious glamor as well as a scholarly stamp of approval. It is in the mountain man of the Rockies in the heyday of the fur trade that we found an archetypal hero emerging, an adventurous figure found in virtually every nationalist account of western man's contact with the undeveloped world.

This particular coloration of the mountain man prevails today in influential monographs and textbooks and indicates that perhaps it is time to make a revaluation of such "pathfinders" as George Croghan, Manuel Lisa, Jedediah Smith, William Ashley, James Ohio Pattie, David Jackson, and the Sublette brothers, who were among the first to begin civilization's war against wildlife on the American continent. If an overdue revaluation

of these men fits them into the classification of some of the "varmints" they cleaned out, then there are others who might be reclassified for recognition among the heroes of American history. We might even want to take a second look at Daniel Boone, Kit Carson, and Jim Bridger, or the great entrepreneur, John Jacob Astor.

It can be argued that we cannot morally condemn the pioneers for exploitation. They acted in a manner consistent with their circumstances within their concepts of territorial rights, justice, and morality. When the sky was darkened by thousands of pigeons, the normal, expected reaction was to kill them off wastefully. What we can blame is the continuation of such attitudes into an era of scarcity. We should understand our pioneers, perhaps, rather than blaming them for what they did.

It can be further argued that the pioneers, who were quite as mercenary as the leaders of large companies, did not understand the long-range consequences of what they were doing to the land. There were few individuals among the farmers, the hydraulic and strip miners, the loggers, or the sheep and cattle men—for that matter, the fur companies and the railroad tycoons—who had any real conception of the vital importance of the resources they were destroying. They did not grasp the significance of muddy streams cleaned of beaver, waterways that had once run deep and clear. Nor did they appreciate the importance of the vital prairie grasses that were plowed under in a few decades. They were often unaware that precious minerals quickly and forever disappeared from our streams and mountains. Indeed, what nineteenth century conservationists talked about the railroads destroying the ecological balance of the Great Plains?

Yet it is not entirely true that the

pioneers, the miners, the fur men, and the western entrepreneurs were ignorant of the consequences of their acts. The pioneer's question, "Why should I look after my descendants?" and his answer, "They ain't done nothin' for me," go back generations in American history. Our ancestors were often intentionally and ruthlessly destructive. In California, for example, the manner and thoroughness in which California's wildlife and groups of aboriginal people were killed is a blackwash on all Americans. The Spaniards and Mexicans of California seemingly were able to live with wildlife without destroying it. But the forty-niners of California's golden age and their followers were wildly wasteful of elk, antelope, bighorns, bears, small fur bearing animals, grouse, geese, and shorebirds. Thousands of dollars were made in selling game meat to miners. In California alone a great faunal shift took place in the years 1850–1910, only duplicated by prehistoric post-glacial terminations of certain species. The California grizzly was pursued until none at all survive today. Here we have a historic example of the dismal story of mass slaughter of wildlife. Alaska faces a somewhat similar crisis today.

The attempt to preserve the wilderness resources left to us surely deserves the support of historians. The old fur trade history was lopsided—unsympathetic to the land and its environment, glorifying the hunter and trapper. It should be rejected by the coming critical generation of American historians. To a degree, the same kind of criticism can be leveled at conventional "frontier" expansion histories of the cattlemen, mining, lumbering, agriculture, business, transportation, industry, and Indians. The assessment will certainly be made; and the sooner it begins, the better. The tunneled frontiersman vision of our past that has engendered a conquistador attitude toward the land will be revised. Our history will surely have new heroes and a new category of destructive varmints. Some historians writing on conservation, Indian history, and related topics have already pointed the way.

The movement to halt the destruction and pollution of the natural environment is now taking root all over the world. We know mankind has now the potential for self-destruction, for irretrievable pollution of the environment as well as for over-crowding the land. American historians either as individuals or working within the framework of our academic organizations . . . can contribute to the success of the movement to bring about a better balance between man and nature by zeroing in on the origins of the destruction of our environment.

A literary historian, LEO MARX (b. 1919) has specialized in understanding the meaning of pastoralism in the American context. His *The Machine in the Garden: Technology and the Pastoral Ideal in America* is a provocative study of the tension in American thought between two sets of priorities. Here Marx explores a larger tension—that between the dominant value structure in the United States and the ecological perspective. What does Marx's analysis suggest about the possibility of solving the environmental crisis?

Leo Marx

Ecology and American Ideals

Anyone familiar with the work of the classic American writers (I am thinking of men like Cooper, Emerson, Thoreau, Melville, Whitman, and Mark Twain) is likely to have developed an interest in what we recently have learned to call ecology. One of the first things we associate with each of the writers just named is a distinctive, vividly particularized setting (or landscape) inseparable from the writer's conception of man. Partly because of the special geographic and political circumstances of American experience, and partly because they were influenced by the romantic vision of man's relations with nature, all of the writers mentioned possessed a heightened sense of place. Yet words like *place, landscape,* or *setting* scarcely can do justice to the significance these writers imparted to external nature in their work. They took for granted a thorough and delicate interpenetration of consciousness and environment. In fact it now seems evident that these gifted writers had begun, more than a century ago, to measure the quality of American life against something like an ecological ideal.

The ideal I have in mind, quite simply, is the maintenance of a healthy life-enhancing interaction between man and the environment. This is layman's language for the proposition that every organism, in order to avoid extinction or expulsion from its ecosystem, must conform to certain minimal requirements of that system. What makes the concept of the ecosystem difficult to grasp, admit-

From Leo Marx, "American Institutions and Ecological Ideals," *Science* (November 27, 1970) Vol. 170, pp. 945–952. Copyright 1970 by the American Association for the Advancement of Science.

tedly, is the fact that the boundaries between systems are always somewhat indistinct, and our technology is making them less distinct all the time. Since an ecosystem includes not only all living organisms (plants and animals) but also the inorganic (physical and chemical) components of the environment, it has become extremely difficult, in the thermonuclear age, to verify even the relatively limited autonomy of local or regional systems. If a decision taken in Moscow or Washington can effect a catastrophic change in the chemical composition of the entire biosphere, then the idea of a San Francisco, or Bay Area, or California, or even North American ecosystem loses much of its clarity and force. Similar difficulties arise when we contemplate the global rate of human population growth. All this is only to say that, on ecological grounds, the case for world government is beyond argument. Meanwhile, we have no choice but to use the nation-states as political instruments for coping with the rapid deterioration of the physical world we inhabit.

The chief question before us, then, is this: What are the prospects, given the character of America's dominant institutions, for the fulfillment of this ecological ideal? But first, what is the significance of the current "environmental crusade"? Why should we be skeptical about its efficacy? How shall we account for the curious response of the scientific community? To answer these questions I will attempt to characterize certain of our key institutions from an ecological perspective. I want to suggest the striking convergence of the scientific and the literary criticism of our national life-style. In conclusion I will suggest a few responses to the ecological crisis indicated by that scientific-literary critique.

In this country, until recently, ecological thinking has been obscured by the more popular, if limited, conservationist viewpoint. Because our government seldom accorded protection of the environment a high priority, much of the responsibility for keeping that end in view fell upon a few voluntary organizations known as the "conservation movement." From the beginning the movement attracted people with enough time and money to enjoy the outdoor life: sportsmen, naturalists (both amateur and professional), and of course property owners anxious to protect the sanctity of their rural or wilderness retreats. As a result, the conservationist cause came to be identified with the special interests of a few private citizens. It seldom, if ever, has been made to seem pertinent to the welfare of the poor, the nonwhite population, or, for that matter, the great majority of urban Americans. The environment that mattered most to conservationists was the environment beyond the city limits. Witness the names of such leading organizations as the Sierra Club, the National Wildlife Federation, the Audubon Society, and the Izaac Walton League. In the view of many conservationists nature is a world that exists apart from, and for the benefit of, mankind.

The ecological perspective is quite different. Its philosophic root is the secular idea that man (including his works—the secondary, or man-made, environment) is wholly and ineluctably embedded in the tissue of natural process. The interconnections are delicate, infinitely complex, never to be severed. If this organic (or holistic) view of nature has not been popular, it is partly because it calls into question many presuppositions of our culture. Even today an excessive interest in this idea of nature carries, as it did in Emerson's and in Jefferson's time, a strong hint of irregularity and possible subversion. (Nowadays it is associated with the antibourgeois defense of the environment expounded by the long-haired "cop-outs" of the youth movement.) Partly in order to counteract these dangerously idealistic notions, American conservationists often have made a point of seeming hard-headed, which is to say, "realistic" or practical. When their aims have been incorporated in national political programs, notably during the administrations of the two Roosevelts, the emphasis has been upon the efficient use of resources under the supervision of well-trained technicians. Whatever the achievements of such programs, as implemented by the admirable if narrowly defined work of such agencies as the National Park Service, the U.S. Forest Service, or the Soil Conservation Service, they did not raise the kinds of questions about our overall capacity for survival that are brought into view by ecology. In this sense, conservationist thought is pragmatic and meliorist in tenor, whereas ecology is, in the purest meaning of the word, radical.

The relative popularity of the conservation movement helps to explain why troubled scientists, many of whom foresaw the scope and gravity of the environmental crisis a long while ago, have had such a difficult time arousing their countrymen. As early as 1864 George Perkins Marsh, sometimes said to be the father of American ecology, warned that the earth was "fast becoming an unfit home for its noblest inhabitant," and that unless men changed their ways it would be reduced "to such a condition of improverished productiveness, of shattered surface, of climatic excess, as to threaten the depravation, barbarism, and perhaps even extinction of the species". No one was listening to Marsh in 1864, and some 80 years later, according to a distinguished naturalist

who tried to convey a similar warning, most Americans still were not listening. "It is amazing," wrote Fairfield Osborn in 1948, "how far one has to travel to find a person, even among the widely informed, who is aware of the processes of mounting destruction that we are inflicting upon our life sources."

But that was 1948, and, as we all know, the situation now is wholly changed. Toward the end of the 1960's there was a sudden upsurge of public interest in the subject. The devastation of the environment and the threat of overpopulation became too obvious to be ignored. A sense of anxiety close to panic seized many people, including politicians and leaders of the communications industry. The mass media began to spread the alarm. Television gave prime coverage to a series of relatively minor yet visually sensational ecological disasters. Once again, as in the coverage of the Vietnam War, the close-up power of the medium was demonstrated. The sight of lovely beaches covered with crude oil, hundreds of dead and dying birds trapped in the viscous stuff, had an incalculable effect upon a mass audience. After years of indifference, the press suddenly decided that the jeremiads of naturalists might be important news, and a whole new vocabulary (*environment, ecology, balance of nature, population explosion,* and so on) entered common speech. Meanwhile, the language of reputable scientists was escalating to a pitch of excitement comparable with that of the most fervent young radicals. Barry Commoner, for example, gave a widely reported speech describing the deadly pollution of California water reserves as a result of the excessive use of nitrates as fertilizer. This method of increasing agricultural productivity, he said, is so disruptive of the chemical balance of soil and water that within a generation it could poison irreparably the water supply of the whole area. The *New York Times* ran the story under the headline: "Ecologist Sees U.S. on Suicidal Course". But it was the demographers and population biologists, worried about behavior even less susceptible to regulatory action, who used the most protentous rhetoric. "We must realize that unless we are extremely lucky," Paul Ehrlich told an audience in the summer of 1969, "everybody will disappear in a cloud of blue steam in 20 years".

To a layman who assumes that responsible scientists choose their words with care, this kind of talk is bewildering. How seriously should he take it? He realizes, of course, that he has no way, on his own, to evaluate the factual or scientific basis for these fearful predictions. But the scientific community, to which he naturally turns, is not much help. While most scientists calmly go about their business, activists like Commoner and Ehrlich dominate the headlines. . . . No—what is bewildering is the disparity between words and action, between the all-too-credible prophets of disaster and the response—or rather the nonresponse—of the organized scientific community. From a layman's viewpoint, the professional scientific organizations would seem to have an obligation here—where nothing less than human survival is in question—either to endorse or to correct the pronouncements of their distinguished colleagues. If a large number of scientists do indeed endorse the judgment of the more vociferous ecologists, then the inescapable question is: What are they doing about it? Why do they hesitate to use the concerted prestige and force of their profession to effect radical changes in national policy and behavior? How is it that most scientists,

in the face of this awful knowledge, if indeed it is knowledge, are able to carry on business more or less as usual? One might have expected them to raise their voices, activate their professional organizations, petition the Congress, send delegations to the President, and speak out to the people and the government. Why, in short, are they not mounting a campaign of education and political action?

The most plausible answer seems to be that many scientists, like many of their fellow citizens, are ready to believe that such a campaign already has begun. And if, indeed, one accepts the version of political reality disseminated by the communications industry, they are correct: the campaign *has* begun. By the summer of 1969 it had become evident that the media were preparing to give the ecological crisis the kind of saturation treatment accorded the civil rights movement in the early 1960's and the anti-Vietnam War protest after that. (Observers made this comparison from the beginning.) Much of the tone and substance of the campaign was set by the advertising business. Thus, a leading teen-age magazine, *Seventeen,* took a full-page ad in the *New York Times* to announce, beneath a picture of a handsome collegiate couple strolling meditatively through autumn leaves, "The environment crusade emphasizes the fervent concerns of the young with our nation's 'quality of life.' Their voices impel us to act now on the mushrooming problems of conservation and ecology". A more skeptical voice might impel us to think about the Madison Avenue strategists who had recognized a direct new path into the lucrative youth market. The "crusade," as they envisaged it, was to be a bland, well-mannered, clean-up campaign, conducted in the spirit of an adolescent love affair and nicely timed to deflect student attention from the disruptive political issues of the 1960's. A national survey of college students confirmed this hope. "Environment May Eclipse Vietnam as College Issue," the makers of the survey reported, and one young man's comment seemed to sum up their findings: "A lot of people are becoming disenchanted with the antiwar movement," he said. "People who are frustrated and disillusioned are starting to turn to ecology." On New Year's Day 1970, the President of the United States joined the crusade. Adapting the doomsday rhetoric of the environmentalists to his own purposes, he announced that "the nineteen-seventies absolutely must be the years when America pays its debt to the past by reclaiming the purity of its air, its waters and our living environment. It is literally now or never".

Under the circumstances, it is understandable that most scientists, like most other people (except for the disaffected minority of college students), have been largely unresponsive to the alarmist rhetoric of the more panicky environmentalists. The campaign to save the environment no longer seems to need their help. Not only have the media been awakened, and with them a large segment of the population, but the President himself, along with many government officials, has been enlisted in the cause. On 10 February 1970, President Nixon sent a special message to the Congress outlining a comprehensive 37-point program of action against pollution. Is it any wonder that the mood at recent meetings of conservationists has become almost cheerful—as if the movement, at long last, really had begun to move? After all, the grim forecasts of the ecologists necessarily have been couched in conditional language, thus: *If* California farmers continue their excessive use of nitrates, *then* the water supply will be irreparably poisoned. But now that the facts have been revealed, and with so much government activity in prospect, may we not assume that disaster will be averted? There is no need, therefore, to take the alarmists seriously—which is only to say that most scientists still have confidence in the capacity of our political leaders, and of our institutions, to cope with the crisis.

But is that confidence warranted by the current "crusade"? Many observers have noted that the President's message was strong in visionary language and weak in substance. He recommended no significant increase in funds needed to implement the program. Coming from a politician with a well-known respect for strategies based on advertising and public relations, this high-sounding talk should make us wary. Is it designed to protect the environment or to assuage anxiety or to distract the antiwar movement or to provide the cohesive force necessary for national unity behind the Republican administration? How can we distinguish the illusion of activity fostered by the media—and the President—from auguries of genuine action? On this score, the frequently invoked parallel of the civil rights and the antiwar movements should give us pause. For, while each succeeded in focusing attention upon a dangerous situation, it is doubtful whether either got us very far along toward the elimination of the danger. At first each movement won spectacular victories, but now, in retrospect, they too look more like ideological than substantive gains. In many ways the situation of blacks in America is more desperate in 1970 than it was in 1960. Similarly, the war in Southeast Asia, far from having been stopped by the peace movement, now threatens to encompass other countries and to continue indefinitely. This is not to imply that the strenuous efforts to end the war or to eradicate racism have been bootless. Some day the whole picture may well look quite different; we may look back on the 1960's as the time when a generation was prepared for a vital transformation of American society.

Nevertheless, scientists would do well to contemplate the example of these recent protest movements. They would be compelled to recognize, for one thing, that, while public awareness may be indispensable for effecting changes in national policy, it hardly guarantees results. In retrospect, indeed, the whole tenor of the civil rights and antiwar campaigns now seems much too optimistic. Neither program took sufficient account of the deeply entrenched, institutionalized character of the collective behavior it aimed to change. If leaders of the campaign to save the environment were to make the same kind of error, it would not be surprising. A certain innocent trust in the efficacy of words, propaganda, and rational persuasion always has characterized the conservation movement in this country. Besides, there is a popular notion that ecological problems are in essence technological, not political, and therefore easier to solve than the problems of racism, war, or imperialism. To indicate why this view is a mistaken one, why in fact it would be folly to discount the urgency of the environmental crisis on these grounds, I now want to consider the fitness of certain dominant American institutions for the fulfillment of the ecological ideal.

Seen from an ecological perspective, a salient characteristic of American society is its astonishing dynamism. Ever since the first European settlements were established on the Atlantic seaboard, our history has been one of virtually uninterrupted expansion. How many decades, if any, have there been since 1607 when this society failed to expand its population, territory, and economic power? When foreigners speak of Americanization they invariably have in mind this dynamic, expansionary, unrestrained behavior. "No sooner do you set foot upon American ground," wrote de Tocqueville, "than you are stunned by a kind of tumult; a confused clamor is heard on every side, and a thousand simultaneous voices demand the satisfaction of their social wants. Everything is in motion around you . . ." To be sure, a majority of these clamorous people were of European origin, and their most effective instrument for the transformation of the wilderness—their science and technology—was a product of Western culture. But the unspoiled terrain of North America gave European dynamism a peculiar effervescence. The seemingly unlimited natural resources and the relative absence of cultural or institutional restraints made possible what surely has been the fastest-developing, most mobile, most relentlessly innovative society in world history. By now that dynamism inheres in every aspect of our lives, from the dominant national ethos to the structure of our economic institutions down to the deportment of individuals.

The ideological counterpart to the nation's physical expansion has been its celebration of quantity. What has been valued most in American popular culture is growth, development, size (bigness), and—by extension—change, novelty, innovation, wealth, and power.

This tendency was noted a long while ago, especially by foreign travelers, but only recently have historians begun to appreciate the special contribution of Christianity to this quantitative, expansionary ethos. The crux here is the aggressive, man-centered attitude toward the environment fostered by Judeo-Christian thought: everything in nature, living or inorganic, exists to serve man. For only man can hope (by joining God) to transcend nature. According to one historian of science, Lynn White, the dynamic thrust of Western science and technology derives in large measure from this Christian emphasis, unique among the great world religions, upon the separation of man from nature.

But one need not endorse White's entire argument to recognize that Americans, from the beginning, found in the Bible a divine sanction for their violent assault upon the physical environment. To the Puritans of New England, the New World landscape was Satan's territory, a hideous wilderness inhabited by the unredeemed and fit chiefly for conquest. What moral precept could have served their purpose better than the Lord's injunction to be fruitful and multiply and subdue the earth and exercise dominion over every living creature? Then, too, the millennial cast of evangelical protestantism made even more dramatic the notion that this earth, and everything upon it, is an expendable support system for man's voyage to eternity. Later as industrialization gained momentum, the emphasis shifted from the idea of nature as the devil's country to the idea of nature as commodity. When the millennial hope was secularized, and salvation was replaced by the goal of economic and social progress, it became possible to quantify the rate of human improvement. In our time this quantifying bent

reached its logical end with the enshrinement of the gross national product—one all-encompassing index of the state of the union itself.

Perhaps the most striking thing about this expansionary ethos, from an ecological viewpoint, has been its capacity to supplant a whole range of common-sense notions about man's relations with nature which are recognized by some preliterate peoples and are implicit in the behavior of certain animal species. These include the ideas that natural resources are exhaustible, that the unchecked growth of a species will eventually lead to its extinction, and that other organisms may have a claim to life worthy of respect.

The record of American business, incomparably successful according to quantitative economic measures like the gross national product, also looks quite different when viewed from an ecological perspective. Whereas the environmental ideal I have been discussing affirms the need for each organism to observe limits set by its ecosystem, the whole thrust of industrial capitalism has been in the opposite direction: it has placed the highest premium upon ingenious methods for circumventing those limits. After comparing the treatment that various nations have accorded their respective portions of the earth, Fairfield Osborn said this of the United States: "The story of our nation in the last century as regards the use of forests, grasslands, wildlife and water sources is the most violent and the most destructive in the long history of civilization." If that estimate is just, a large part of the credit must be given to an economic system unmatched in calling forth man's profit-making energies. By the same token, it is a system that does pitifully little to encourage or reward those constraints necessary for the long-term ecological well-being of society. Consider, for example, the fate of prime agricultural lands on the borders of our burgeoning cities. What happens when a landowner is offered a small fortune by a developer? What agency protects the public interest from the irretrievable loss of topsoil that requires centuries to produce? Who sees to it that housing, factories, highways, and shopping centers are situated on the far more plentiful sites where nothing edible ever will grow? The answer is that no such agencies exist, and the market principle is allowed to rule. Since World War II approximately one-fifth of California's invaluable farm land has been lost in this way. Here, as in many cases of air and water pollution, the dominant motive of our business system—private profit—leads to the violation of ecological standards.

Early in the industrial era one might reasonably have expected, as Thorstein Veblen did, that the scientific and technological professions, with their strong bent toward rationality and efficiency, would help to control the ravening economic appetites whetted by America's natural abundance. Veblen assumed that well-trained technicians, engineers, and scientists would be repelled by the wastefulness of the business system. He therefore looked to them for leadership in shaping alternatives to a culture obsessed with "conspicuous consumption." But, so far, that leadership has not appeared. On the contrary, this new technical elite, with its commitment to highly specialized, value-free research, has enthusiastically placed its skill in the service of business and military enterprise. This is one reason, incidentally, why today's rebellious young are unimpressed by the claim that the higher learning entails a commitment to rationality. They see our best-educated, most "rational" elite serving what strikes them as a higher irrationality. So far from providing a counterforce to the business system, the scientific and technological professions in fact have strengthened the ideology of American corporate capitalism, including its large armaments sector, by bringing to it their high-minded faith in the benign consequences of the most rapidly accelerating rate of technological innovation attainable.

But not only are we collectively committed, as a nation, to the idea of continuing growth; each subordinate unit of the society holds itself to a similar standard of success. Each state, city, village, and neighborhood; each corporation, independent merchant, and voluntary organization; each ethnic group, family, and child—each person—should ideally speaking, strive for growth. Translated into ecological terms, this popular measure of success—becoming bigger, richer, more powerful—means gaining control over more and more of the available resources. When resources were thought to be inexhaustible, as they were thought to be throughout most of our national history, the release of these unbounded entrepreneurial energies was considered an aspect of individual liberation. And so it was, at least for large segments of the population. But today, when that assumption no longer makes sense, those energies are still being generated. It is as if a miniaturized version of the nation's expansionary ethos had been implanted in every citizen—not excluding the technicians and scientists. And when we consider the extremes to which the specialization of function has been carried in the sciences, each expert working his own minuscule sector of the knowledge industry, it is easier to account for the unresponsiveness of the scientific community to the urgent warnings of alarmed ecologists. If most scientists and engineers seem not to be listening, much less acting, it is because these highly skilled men are so busy doing what every good American is supposed to do.

On the other hand, it is not surprising that a clever novelist like Norman Mailer or a popular interpreter of science like Rachel Carson or an imaginative medical researcher like Alan Gregg each found it illuminating in recent years to compare the unchecked growth of American society, with all the resulting disorder, to the haphazard spread of cancer cells in a living organism. There is nothing new, of course, about the analogy between the social order and the human body; the conceit has a long history in literature. Since the early 1960's, however, Mailer has been invoking the more specific idea of America as a carcinogenic environment. Like any good poetic figure, this one has a basis in fact. Not only does it call to mind the radioactive matter we have deposited in the earth and the sea, or the work of such allegedly cancer-producing enterprises as the tobacco and automobile industries, or the effects of some of the new drugs administered by doctors in recent years, but, even more subtly, it reminds us of the parallel between cancer and our expansionary national ethos, which, like a powerful ideological hormone, stimulates the reckless, uncontrolled growth of each cell in the social organism.

In the interests of historical accuracy and comprehensiveness, needless to say, all of these sweeping generalizations would have to be extensively qualified. The record is rich in accounts of determined, troubled Americans who have critized and actively resisted the nation's expansionary abandon. A large part of our governmental apparatus was created in order to keep these acquisitive, self-aggrandizing energies within tolerable limits. And of course the full story would acknowledge the obvious benefits, especially the individual freedom and prosperity, many Americans owe to the very dynamism that now threatens our survival. But in this brief compass my aim is to emphasize that conception of man's relation to nature which, so far as we can trace its consequences, issued in the *dominant* forms of national behavior. And that is a largely one-sided story. It is a story, moreover, to which our classic American writers, to their inestimable credit, have borne eloquent witness. If there is a single native institution which has consistently criticized American life from a vantage like that of ecology, it is the institution of letters.

A notable fact about imaginative literature in America, when viewed from an ecological perspective, is the number of our most admired works written in obedience to a pastoral impulse. By "pastoral impulse" I mean the urge, in the face of society's increasing power and complexity, to retreat in the direction of nature. The most obvious form taken by this withdrawal from the world of established institutions is a movement in space. The writer or narrator describes, or a character enacts, a move away from a relatively sophisticated to a simpler, more "natural" environment. Whether this new setting is an unspoiled wilderness, like Cooper's forests and plains, Melville's remote Pacific, Faulkner's Big Woods, or Hemingway's Africa, or whether it is as tame as Emerson's New England village common, Thoreau's Walden Pond, or Robert Frost's pasture, its significance derives from the plain fact that it is "closer" to nature: it is a landscape that bears fewer marks of human intervention.

This symbolic action, which reenacts

the initial transit of Europeans to North America, may be understood in several ways, and no one of them can do it justice. To begin with, there is an undeniable element of escapism about this familiar, perhaps universal, desire to get away from the imperatives of a complicated social life. No one has conveyed this feeling with greater economy or simplicity than Robert Frost in the first line of his poem "Directive": "Back out of all this now too much for us." Needless to say, if our literary pastoralism lent expression only to this escapist impulse, we would be compelled to call it self-indulgent, puerile, or regressive.

But fortunately this is not the case. In most American pastorals the movement toward nature also may be understood as a serious criticism, explicit or implied, of the established social order. It calls into question a society dominated by a mechanistic system of value, keyed to perfecting the routine means of existence, yet oblivious to its meaning and purpose. We recall Thoreau's description, early in *Walden,* of the lives of quiet desperation led by his Concord neighbors, or the first pages of Melville's *Moby-Dick,* with Ishmael's account of his moods of suicidal depression as he contemplates the meaningless work required of the inhabitants of Manhattan Island. At one time this critical attitude toward the workaday life was commonly dismissed as aristocratic or elitist. We said that it could speak only for a leisure class for whom deprivation was no problem. But today, in a society with the technological capacity to supply everyone with an adequate standard of living, that objection has lost most of its force. The necessary conditions for giving a decent livelihood to every citizen no longer include harder work, increased productivity, or endless technological innovation. But of course

such an egalitarian economic program would entail a more equitable distribution of wealth, and the substitution of economic sufficiency for the goal of an endlessly "rising" standard of living. The mere fact that such possibilities exist explains why our literary pastorals, which blur distinctions between the economic, moral, and esthetic flaws of society, now seem more cogent. In the 19th century, many pastoralists, like today's radical ecologists, saw the system as potentially destructive in its innermost essence. Their dominant figure for industrial society, with its patent confusion about ends and means, was the social machine. Our economy is the kind of system, said Thoreau, where men become the tools of their tools.

Of course, there is nothing particularly American about this pessimistic literary response to industrialism. Since the romantic movement it has been a dominant theme of all Western literature. Most gifted writers have expended a large share of their energy in an effort to discover—or, more precisely, to imagine—alternatives to the way of life that emerged with the industrial revolution. The difference is that in Europe there was a range of other possible lifestyles which had no counterpart in this country. There were enclaves of preindustrial culture (provincial, esthetic, religious, aristocratic) which retained their vitality long after the bourgeois revolutions, and there also was a new, revolutionary, urban working class. This difference, along with the presence in America of a vast, rich, unspoiled landscape, helps to explain the exceptionally strong hold of the pastoral motive upon the native imagination. If our writers conceived of life from something like an ecological perspective, it is largely because of their heightened sensitivity to the unspoiled environment, and man's relation to it, as the basis for an alternative to the established social order.

What, then, can we learn about possible alternatives from our pastoral literature? The difficulty here lies in the improbability which surrounds the affirmative content of the pastoral retreat. In the typical American fable the high point of the withdrawal toward nature is an idyllic interlude which gains a large measure of its significance from the sharp contrast with the everyday, "real," world. This is an evanescent moment of peace and contentment when the writer (or narrator, or protagonist) enjoys a sense of integration with the surrounding environment that approaches ecstatic fulfillment. It is often a kind of visionary experience, couched in a language of such intense, extreme, even mystical feeling that it is difficult for many readers (though not, significantly, for adherents of today's youth culture) to take it seriously. But it is important to keep in view some of the reasons for this literary extravagance. In a commercial, optimistic, self-satisfied culture, it was not easy for writers to make an alternate mode of experience credible. Their problem was to endow an ideal vison—some would call it utopian—with enough sensual authenticity to carry readers beyond the usual, conventionally accepted limits of commonsense reality. Nevertheless, the pastoral interlude, rightly understood, does have a bearing upon the choices open to a postindustrial society. It must be taken, not as representing a program to be copied, but as a symbolic action which embodies values, attitudes, modes of thought and feeling alternative to those which characterize the dynamic, expansionary life-style of modern America.

The focus of our literary pastoralism, accordingly, is upon a contrast between two environments representing virtually all aspects of man's relation to nature. In place of the aggressive thrust of 19th-century capitalism, the pastoral interlude exemplifies a far more restrained, accommodating kind of behavior. The chief goal is not, as Alexander Hamilton argued it was, to enhance the nation's corporate wealth and power; rather it is the Jeffersonian "pursuit of happiness." In economic terms, then, pastoralism entails a distinction between a commitment to unending growth and the concept of material sufficiency. The aim of the pastoral economy is *enough*—enough production and consumption to insure a decent quality of life. Jefferson's dislike of industrialization was based on this standard; he was bent on the subordination of quantitative to qualitative "standards of living."

From a psychological viewpoint, the pastoral retreat affirmed the possibility of maintaining man's mental equilibrium by renewed emphasis upon his inner needs. The psychic equivalent of the balance of nature (in effect the balance of *human* nature) is a more or less equal capacity to cope with external and internal sources of anxiety. In a less-developed landscape, according to these fables, behavior can be more free, spontaneous, authentic—in a word, more natural. The natural in psychic experience refers to activities of mind which are inborn or somehow primary. Whether we call them intuitive, unconscious, or preconscious, the significant fact is that they do not have to be learned or deliberately acquired. By contrast, then, the expansionary society is figured forth as dangerously imbalanced on the side of those rational faculties conducive to the manipulation of the physical environment. We think of Melville's Ahab, in whom the specialization of function induces a peculiar kind of power-obsessed, if technically competent, mentality. "My means are sane," he says, "my motive and my object mad."

This suspicion of the technical, highly trained intellect comports with the emphasis in our pastoral literature upon those aspects of life that are common to all men. Whereas the industrial society encourages and rewards the habit of mind which analyzes, separates, categorizes, and makes distinctions, the felicity enjoyed during the pastoral interlude is a tacit tribute to the opposite habit. This kind of pleasure derives from the connection-making, analogizing, poetic imagination —one that aspires to a unified conception of reality. At the highest or metaphysical level of abstraction, then, romantic pastoralism is holistic. During the more intense pastoral interludes, an awareness of the entire environment, extending to the outer reaches of the cosmos, affects the perception of each separate thing, idea, event. In place of the technologically efficient but limited concept of nature as a body of discrete manipulatable objects, our pastoral literature presents an organic conception of man's relation to his environment.

What I am trying to suggest is the striking convergence of the literary and the ecological views of America's dominant institutions. Our literature contains a deep intuition of the gathering environmental crisis and its causes. To be sure, the matter-of-fact idiom of scientific ecology may not be poetic or inspiring. Instead of conveying Wordsworthian impulses from the vernal wood, it reports the rate at which monoxide poisoning is killing the trees. Nevertheless, the findings of ecologists confirm the indictment of the self-aggrandizing way of life that our leading writers have been building up for almost two centuries. In essence it is an indictment of the destructive, power-oriented uses to which we put scientific and technological knowledge. The philosophic source of this dangerous behavior is an arrogant conception of man, and above all of human consciousness, as wholly unique—as an entity distinct from, and potentially independent of, the rest of nature.

As for the alternative implied by the pastoral retreat, it also anticipates certain insights of ecology. Throughout this body of imaginative writing, the turn toward nature is represented as a means of gaining access to governing values, meanings, and purposes. In the past, to be sure, many readers found the escapist, sentimental overtones of this motive embarrassing. As a teacher, I can testify that, until recently, many pragmatically inclined students were put off by the obscurely metaphysical, occultish notions surrounding the idea of harmony with nature. It lacked specificity. But now all that is changing. The current environmental crisis has in a sense put a literal, factual, often quantifiable base under this poetic idea. Nature as a transmitter of signals and a dictator of choices now is present to us in the quite literal sense that the imbalance of an ecosystem, when scientifically understood, defines certain percise limits to human behavior. We are told, for example, that if we continue contaminating Lake Michigan at the present rate, the lake will be "dead" in roughly 10 years. Shall we save the lake or continue allowing the cities and industries which pollute it to reduce expenses and increase profits? As such choices become more frequent, man's relations with nature will in effect be seen to set the limits of various economic, social, and political practices. And the concept of harmonious relations between man and the physical environment, instead of seeming to be a vague projection of human wishes, must come to be respected as a necessary, realistic, limiting goal. This convergence of literary and scientific insight reinforces the naturalistic idea that man, to paraphrase Melville, must eventually lower his conceit of attainable felicity, locating it not in power or transcendence but in a prior need to sustain life itself.

Assuming that this sketch of America's dominant institutions as seen from a pastoral-ecological vantage is not grossly inaccurate, what inferences can we draw from it? What bearing does it have upon our current effort to cope with the deterioration of the environment? What special significance does it have for concerned scientists and technologists? . . .

Scientists and technologists, as an organized professional group, must become more actively involved. It was scientists, after all, who first sounded the alarm. What action we take as a society *and how quickly we take it* depend in large measure upon the credibility of the alarmists. Who is to say, if organized science does not, which alarms we should take seriously? What group has anything like the competence of scientists and technologists to evaluate the evidence? Or, to put it negatively, what group can do more, by mere complacency and inaction, to insure an inadequate response to the environmental crisis? It is a well-known fact that Americans hold the scientific profession in the highest esteem. So long as most scientists go about their business as usual, so long as they seem unperturbed by the urgent appeals of their own colleagues, it is likely that most laymen, including our political representatives, will remain skeptical.

The arguments for the more active involvement of the scientific community in public debate illustrate the all-encompassing and essentially political character of the environmental crisis. If the literary-ecological perspective affords an accurate view, we must eventually take into account the deep-seated, institutional causes of our distress. No cosmetic program, no clean-up-the-landscape activity, no degree of protection for the wilderness, no antipollution laws can be more than the merest beginning. Of course such measures are worthwhile, but in undertaking them we should acknowledge their superficiality. The devastation of the environment is at bottom a result of the kind of society we have built and the kind of people we are. It follows, therefore, that environmentalists should join forces, wherever common aims can be found, with other groups concerned to change basic institutions. To arrest the deterioration of the environment it will be necessary to control many of the same forces which have prevented us from ending the war in Indochina or giving justice to black Americans. In other words, it will be necessary for ecologists to determine where the destructive power of our society lies and how to cope with it. Knowledge of that kind, needless to say, is political. But then it seems obvious, on reflection, that the study of human ecology will be incomplete until it incorporates a sophisticated mode of political analysis.

Meanwhile, it would be folly, given the character of American institutions, to discount the urgency of our situation either on the ground that technology will provide the solutions or on the ground that countermeasures are proposed. We cannot rely on technology because the essential problem is not technological. It inheres in all of the ways in which this dynamic society generates and uses its power. It calls into question the controlling purposes of all the major institutions which actually determine the nation's impact upon the environment: the great business corporations, the military establishment, the universities, the scientific and technological elites, and the exhilarating expansionary ethos by which we all live. Throughout our brief history, a passion for personal and collective aggrandizement has been the American way. One can only guess at the extent to which forebodings of ecological doom have contributed to the revulsion that so many intelligent young people feel these days for the idea of "success" as a kind of limitless ingestion. In any case, most of the talk about the environmental crisis that turns on the word *pollution,* as if we face a cosmic-scale problem of sanitation, is grossly misleading. What confronts us is an extreme imbalance between society's hunger—the rapidly growing sum of human wants—and the limited capacities of the earth.

For ecologist RAYMOND DASMANN (b. 1919) the history of man's impact on the environment of California has been an unrelieved nightmare. After discussing it for ten chapters in his book, Dasmann used this, his concluding chapter, to express his personal fears and hopes. Of course the specifics in his account pertain to a single state, but they could be extended to any of America's fifty. What do you think is the value of studying their histories and that of the nation as a whole in terms of environment? Is the past a guide to the future? If so, what conclusions can you draw from the material assembled in this book?

Raymond Dasmann

The Destruction of California

I know a girl who maintains that her whole life has been haunted by the vision of a place called Cherry Street. It is a dreamland, she says, formed from reading too many public school books about Dick, Jane, Sally, and their like. In their world everybody is always pleasant and kind. They all live in nice houses with friendly neighbors. There is no trouble or violence, no social nastiness or antagonistic cooperation, no race problems or wars. My own equivalent is a place called California. Once I thought that I lived there. Now I know it no longer exists, and suspect that it was always a dream. Perhaps it resulted from staring too long at the waves breaking on the coast, and thinking back, as the song goes, "on all the tales you can remember—of Camelot."

Yet, at some times in some places I still feel this place called California around me, but the times come more seldom and the places are farther apart. More do I wonder, nowadays, if such a world can be created by man. The practically minded tell me No. But the "roots of heaven" reach into men's hearts, and one must dream.

Is it really too much to ask people to be concerned with the land in which they live? Is it too much to ask them to question those measures that come before city council or state legislature in the light of what effects they will have on their land? The dams on the Trinity [River] are their concern. They will not only change the Trinity; they will bring more people to Southern California and irrigate more desert land. Perhaps some people think there are enough people in Southern California, and like to see deserts as deserts. If so, they had better watch the Trinity. The freeways that threaten to cut the heart out of San Francisco and destroy areas that all of us once thought were loved, cherished, and safe are surely everyone's concern, even if most people rarely visit the cities or places involved. The power of the State Highway Commission to condemn land can be curtailed if the people want it. Is it more important to "get there fast" or to have some place worth going to?

There are many areas in California that are underpopulated, just as there are those that are seriously overpopulated. With underpopulation the social amenities are lacking and cultural advantages are absent, even though wild land resources are abundant. With adequate planning it is possible to increase the population, to gain the cultural and social advantages, and still to preserve the wild country. It is everyone's concern to see that this is done, rather than have people continue to pile up in unsuitable locations.

Conservation is everybody's business. But what goes under that name today is often a piecemeal, stopgap activity that is often too late, and usually too little. It stands too often in the path of what is called progress, and thus arouses the ire of those concerned with moneymaking. Conservationists find themselves always in the desperate position of trying to impose some control over an activity that is already underway, or of trying to save some piece of land or scenery against the opposition of powerful pressure groups. Always their activities seem beside the point to those involved in the main business of our society.

A newspaper such as the *San Francisco Chronicle,* which has featured conserva-

tion news and played a role in the fight to preserve natural beauty in California, still must devote 90 percent of its news space to items that are at best only tangentially related to conservation. Is it that people are not interested in their environment and do not care much about conservation matters? The answer is obviously No. Too many people visit state and national parks, hunt or fish in national forests, join organizations dedicated to civic improvement, for one to say that they lack interest. Yet conservation often seems to lack urgency, to be peripheral to the main business of life. A crisis in Vietnam drives the most pressing conservation problems from the paper. The prospect of world destruction through nuclear war, stemming from the acceptance of an insane outlook on international affairs, can always drive matters concerning world improvement from the headlines. The exploration of outer space, a scientific exercise that seems to hold little relevance to our earthly problems, also captures headlines because of its relation to missilery, weapons, and international conflicts. We don't really want to spend billions for a handful of moon dust, only to see that the Russians don't grab it first. Basically the world crises that compel our attention are related to natural resource and population problems. Well-fed, well-clothed people who are integrated with their physical and social environment don't normally threaten their neighbors. Racial violence and unrest at home drive even international crises from the news. Again a basis can be found in conservation matters. A properly planned city with adequate opportunity for all would not breed the strife and turmoil that emanates from a Harlem or a Fillmore district.

My definition of conservation includes the ecology of man's environment and the social organizations that he uses to achieve a state of well-being within that environment. Conservation problems thus range from city organization to the preservation of wilderness areas. To me they cannot be dissociated. We cannot save a wilderness or a wild species without paying attention to the problems of life in the cities; we cannot have a satisfactory life in a city without having wild country and wildlife accessible on the horizon. We cannot plan for land and resources without consideration of human population problems. In California today, conservation problems, as so defined, are paramount.

The critical problem in California today is that of population increase. This is also the most important problem in the world today, but the California problem has a different aspect. The state is not threatened so much by a runaway birth rate, although this is involved, as it is by a runaway immigration rate. Birthrates have been declining in recent years. The use of new contraceptive chemicals and devices, and the widespread public awareness of population problems, have shown signs of bringing birthrates, as such, under control. But how, in a democratic society, can you prevent people from moving to the place where they want to live? We cannot insist upon a passport and visa for prospective visitors to California.

There are various answers to the problem of controlling population increase in California. One is relatively simple, and involves *not* planning for population growth. This means not encouraging new industries to move into an area. It means not developing our water resources to a maximum, and thus not providing the water that would make possible additional urban or industrial growth, or bring into production new farming areas. It means not building those new power stations or those new freeways. No real-estate de-

velopment will be built in an area where electricity and water will not be provided. No industry will come where it will not receive space, power, or water. People will not come where there are no new jobs or new housing, or if they do come they will not stay. Immigration is not excluded, but the immigrants will be a minority willing to compete for existing jobs and housing space.

The idea of controlling population increase by not providing for it, and indeed forbidding the development of new facilities, is not original. It has been used already, on a small scale. One of the most charming places in California is the city of Santa Barbara. It has maintained its quiet beauty by excluding the kind of industrial growth that other cities have welcomed. It has not allowed housing sprawl. It has fought the State Highway Commission and its monstrous freeway system to a halt, temporarily at least. The continuing charm of the Carmel region, farther north, has been maintained by a firm and definite stand against "progress" by its residents. But these are small places, inhabited by the wealthy. It is most unlikely that active discouragement of population increase on a statewide scale will be tried out. It goes against the entire philosophy of the expanding economy. Too many people look forward to population growth, even while they decry its effects, for them to accept a plan for its discouragement. Such a plan would mean that all those who had invested in land would find land values no longer increasing. It would say to those in business and industry that they could expect no further expansion of the California market. All of us are too used to being pushed to higher levels by people crowding in from below to accept the idea that growth and expansion have ended.

Because the solution of conservation

problems demands a rejection of the expanding economy concept, most people will have ambiguous attitudes toward conservation issues. Many people will vote for a national park because only a few will have invested in the lands or resources to be included within that park. Those that have such investments may oppose that particular park, although they may be advocates of parks in general. Hardly anyone wants to see a nuclear-power plant on a scenic headland, but too many people own stocks in the power company, own land that can be increased in value when more power becomes available, or have shares in industries that require more power, for the opposition to its construction to gain an easy victory. I may favor a lessened rate of utilization of forest resources, but would howl loudly if my book could not be published because of a shortage of paper. Thus, although I am inclined to favor a Redwood National Park* I sympathize deeply with Arcata Redwood Company, whose lands are involved. Support for conservation measures is therefore erratic, and the curtailment of population growth necessary to reach a real solution for our problems is generally inacceptable. Our very economic system prevents our doing the things needed to protect our environment from destruction, and we are sadly aware that other alternative economic systems in existence today work no better.

However, since we are facing this problem it is not fair to avoid looking at the whole picture. What is the alternative to our failure to curtail population growth? We must then plan for population increase and work with all our ability to provide for it. We must harness all available power, develop all available water resources, utilize forests, range, and farmland to a maximum, use more and more

land for housing developments. We must look forward to a monstrous supercity extending from San Diego to the Tehachapis and slopping over into the deserts, and another one extending from the Sierra foothills to San Francisco's peninsula, and reaching northward into the Sonoma and Napa valleys, and southward to Carmel. But perhaps before these are fully developed we will begin to run out of some essential. Water is the most likely to run short, even with seawater conversion. No matter how much ingenuity and technological skill we employ, some resource is going to run out and prevent further development. When this happens—and it may come fairly soon—we shall have then reached the absolute limits of possible growth. We must then face up to the problems that were evaded earlier. The expanding economy can then expand no more; populations can grow no further; and a way must be found for reorganizing and living with existing numbers within existing means. But, by then, what a wretched place California will be!

It seems somehow more realistic to recognize now the limits of growth and take measures to adjust to them. Is it not more reasonable to slow down now, and not go full speed ahead until we hit the stone wall that must inevitably stop us? It is perhaps not reasonable to attempt to stop population growth all at once, but it is unreasonable to do nothing about it. Instead, while we still have wild mountains and forests, rangelands and deserts, scenic vistas of parks and reserves, wild animals and space for free people, we should start putting the brakes on further expansion. We can do it by not channeling those last wild rivers, by not building those extra power plants, by not issuing building permits for all those new suburbs. There are many effective ways that growth can be slowed, that massive im-

---

*It was established in 1968.—Ed.

migration can be discouraged, that will not disrupt the economy of the state. Finding these ways and putting them into effect should be the job of state and local governments, and should underly all the regional planning that is going on today.

Whether or not we accept the curtailment of population growth as a primary goal, we must continue to do something about the other subsidiary conservation problems. The most urgent of these is the reorganization of the cities. Since most of California's people are city people, these areas must be tackled first if any order is to be achieved in the state as a whole. Like most people who are supporters of wilderness and wild country, I spend far more time in cities than I do in wilderness. Unlike most of my fellow wild-land ecologists, I like cities, particularly big ones. Anyone who has read this far realizes my feelings toward San Francisco. I am sorry that I cannot like Los Angeles, but it is too formless and sprawling, rather like the San Francisco Bay area with the city of San Francisco removed. I am captivated by some of its environs. At Laguna Beach and Malibu, in Newport-Balboa and in the Palos Verdes development it has some of the most exceedingly beautiful living areas in the world. But behind these pleasant communities sits the vast ugly mass of disorganized industrial development around Wilmington and into Long Beach, the squalor of the decaying Venice region, the pressure of millions of people and cars, the snarl and confusion of the freeways. San Diego, by contrast, is a city where the physical setting has encouraged the development of unusually charming places to live, and the sheer mass of the city is not so great as to defy orderly planning. Through careful control of future growth and redevelopment it could lead all other California cities in

urban beauty. The valley cities have always seemed wretched places to me, and I have resented every visit to the formless confusion that marks Sacramento, and the heat-deadened dullness of Fresno and Bakersfield. But these cities, in recent years, have been striving toward urban beauty. Fresno has reshaped its downtown area and has taken the courageous step of excluding the automobile from its central area.

At one time . . . I favored the idea that city and countryside must be made to flow together, in order to preserve the advantages of both. However, since visiting the cities of Europe, and doing some further reading and thinking on the subject, I have been inclined to change this viewpoint. L. Dudley Stamp, in his book *Applied Geography,* helps to focus thinking on this subject. Lewis Mumford, in his momumental work *The City in History,* provides more substance. Most confirmed urbanities like cities because they are distinct and different from village, small town, or rural area. They provide the happy anonymity and sense of freedom that comes from *not* knowing your neighbor. They have the rush and confusion that comes from diverse people purposefully pursuing their varied activities. They provide long nights when the lights sparkle and the sidewalks are not rolled up. They allow the activities and groups that can spring up only when populations begin to number in hundreds of thousands and members of minorities can come together in sufficient numbers to bolster one another. Parks and green places remain an essential part of all worthwhile cities, but too much integration of city and country can destroy the advantages of both.

I could not begin to plan a city, let alone one that would preserve those qualities of life that are essential to urbanity.

But I hope that those now engaged in tearing down and rebuilding the cities of California will have these qualities in mind. Unfortunately, I see too much evidence that they are not being considered. The remolding of our cities to accommodate the freeway and the parking lot, the capitulation to the demands of the automobile, can destroy the integrity of any city. The central city at least should be built to the scale of a man traveling on foot. The central portions of London, Paris, Rome, and New York invite exploration on foot. I did not feel the need for a motorcar in Europe's cities, but the moment I reached California once more I felt stranded without one.

It is cheering to hear that a new "return to the city" is under way and that the great exodus to the suburbs may be at an end. However, such a move places a greater responsibility on the city authorities to control the mass of new construction that has already been begun. One hopes that a situation can be achieved such as has been approached in London, where a high percentage of people both live and work within a single borough or district of the city. In particular it would be well to see residential buildings going up on some of the downtown city sections. By locating hotels and apartments, restaurants and clubs in such areas, they can be kept alive at night. Today there are large sections of the central city that teem with people in the daylight, but die after dark. Location of living and playing space in such areas would further cut down on the need for transportation through the cities. The development of adequate, rapid public transportation systems could save the central city from the automobile blight. That this is needed is obvious to all, and it is discouraging to see further development of misplaced freeways using funds that could as well

go to a more sensible transportation network.

The necessity for controlling the suburban sprawl has attracted the attention of most people, and is exercising the minds of all concerned with regional planning. It is not practical to eliminate the existing suburbs, but it is possible to organize them into urban centers distinct and separate from the original cities that spawned them. Most particularly we need to set bounds on further suburban development, protecting our high-quality farming lands from additional encroachment. The development of new urban centers within present suburban areas can allow for internal expansion of residential space and further cut down on the need for commuting to some distant center for work. This process, fortunately, is already at work in California; although the continuing spread of suburbs does still go on. Strict county zoning laws are badly needed to prevent the spreading growth of the ugly urban fringe areas that surround and connect both city and suburb . . . the area of billboard and junkyard, used-car lot and shacktown that makes the approach to any city discouraging.

It is easy to write these things, and my repetition of them here simply adds to the volumes of words already written. It seems incredibly difficult to put them into operation, even when the need is obvious. The small entrepreneur who wants to build his pizza parlor, fruit stand, or used-car lot in the orange groves outside the city limits still seems to have undue support from the county authorities. One of my friends, for example, has just waged a three-year fight to prevent the establishment of a crowded trailer park in what had been a first-class residential suburb. After endless hearings and legal wrangles, he lost the struggle, even though one would expect that any rational system of zoning would have supported his point of view. There are those who wish to maintain the right to exploit for a profit regardless of public interest. They still have authority. Those who would fight them fail to attract the support of fellow citizens who live in one place, work someplace else, play in a third place, and feel no community responsibility toward any of the areas concerned. Our dispersed way of living does not lead to the development of interest or pride in a single community. It is to the interest of the quick-profit developers to keep such pride in place from growing.

Moving away from city and suburb, a principal problem for California remains that of transportation facilities. Crowded two-lane highways give way to freeways that eat into farm and forest, towns and parks. Soon the freeways in turn are crowded, and traffic slows to a crawl. We build larger freeways, while population grows and more people buy more cars. More land is destroyed; the new superhighway is again crowded; and a new cycle of enlargement and land destruction begins. In desperation more and more people take to the air, and the growth of airfields encroaches on still more land. The problem of getting from airport to destination becomes as great as that of driving the entire distance to begin with. Meanwhile alternate forms of transportation are neglected. Railroads, which were far less space consuming than highways, fall into neglect, routes are abandoned, and service becomes infrequent. Yet, if attention were given to the problem, a fast, efficient, and comfortable system of rail transportation could surely be devised, and would cost less than the million dollars a mile we are pouring into new freeways. Yet we go on spending hundreds of millions on highway de-velopment, building a choking network of automobile roads. Admittedly the people, through their legislatures, have approved it. But did they know what they were approving? Were they offered any reasonable alternative? Most Americans like automobiles, but all have an inner feeling that driving them should be a pleasure. In California, pleasure driving is becoming an activity to be read about in history books, not a possibility for today.

The problems of California rural lands and wild country, apart from those imposed by urban sprawl and highway encroachment, are largely those of conflicting demands for an ever-shrinking quantity of space and for the water that can make that space usable. As a small, but highly important, segment of these problems are those related to parks and reserves, wilderness and wildlife. Like Morel and his supporters in Romain Gary's *The Roots of Heaven,* I believe that wild animal life and wild country is a bulwark of, and essential to, human freedom. So long as we have space where the wild game herds can wander undisturbed, we have a margin in which individual liberty can thrive. When we chain and confine all our wild country, eliminate the free-roaming animal life, then there will be no space left for that last wild thing, the free human spirit. The machine civilization we have built will have triumphed over us, and we shall have become mere numbers to be organized and moved about by computers. Aldo Leopold once wrote: "I am glad I shall never be young without wild country to be young in. Of what avail are forty freedoms without a blank spot on the map?" There are no blank spots on the California map, but there is still wild country. If it goes, much of meaning of the word "humanity" will go with it. We shall need a new word for the confined creatures that take the place of free men.

At a recent meeting on conservation problems, a resource economist described the necessity for putting a price tag on wildlife and wild country. If wildlife is to maintain a place in competition for land and water we must know its economic value, what the public will pay in order to keep it. He suggested that a step toward achieving this end would be an increase in the cost of hunting and fishing licenses, and presumably also of the fees for access to private lands for hunting and fishing. By such an increase we could get a better measurement of the value attached to our wildlife resources, and could use these figures in bargaining for such things as an allotment of water for a duck marsh or the reservation of lands for public hunting and fishing. While I agree that we need better measurements in economic terms of the values of wild land and wildlife, and have done some work toward attaining such measurements, I cannot agree that current price tags would be a true measure of worth to society. The value of a previously unexploited raw material—uranium ore is an example— cannot be known until its usefulness to society has been demonstrated. A realistic price for a new kind of manufactured product often cannot be set until a public demand for it has become established, usually through advertising its qualities. We cannot establish the value of a remote wilderness area, known to very few people, by determining the price that people will pay today to maintain it. People who know little about wild nature—and city people often have little opportunity to learn—cannot be expected to pay a high price for its maintenance. Yet, unless it is maintained, their understanding will come too late. Like the American Indians, they will have given away gold in ex-

change for glass beads. Aldo Leopold, in his *A Sand County Almanac,* touched on this problem years ago, saying that rather than building roads into the wilderness, we should be building new pathways of understanding into the still unlovely human mind. Such pathways are being built today. In a year of politics and crises, we can still have a wilderness-preservation bill enacted by Congress. But it is still too early to defend priceless aesthetic resources, reservoirs of human freedom, entirely in economic terms. Even highway engineers and water developers must be made to recognize that.

It is possible to stop, here in the West, the destruction of the land that is called California. It is not only possible; it is essential to do so. Ten years hence we shall regret every mistake we are making today, feel deeply the hurt caused by each failure to act. Admittedly we are trying hard to remedy past damage and prevent future loss. Few areas have so many planning agencies as California. Few have so many public and private organizations devoted to the maintenance of the wild scene and natural beauty of their country. Yet there is continuing failure and confusion Some lack of integration in our efforts seems apparent. The pressures of economic growth and population sweep over the little plans of those who are seeking to preserve some space or enhance some natural beauty. The city planners seem to strive in vain against those whose activities would destroy the integrity of the city. Those building a state park system seem to operate in ignorance of the plans of other agencies that would destroy it. We cannot afford to have the various organizations and groups engaged in either preservation or development working in isolation from one another. The kind of wrangle that has gone on for years over Bodega Head or that threatens to go on over the state's Prairie Creek Redwood Park reflects some failure to get the interested groups together at an early enough stage. A long-term answer to the problem of California can come only through full consideration of the total environment within the state. From cities to wilderness plans must be coordinated.

The future of California actually rests in the hands of a relatively small number of groups of people that are involved in the protection of its resources or in their development or exploitation for profit. Half of the land is in federal or state control. Two agencies, the United States Forest Service and the Bureau of Land Management, exercise the major control and bear the greatest responsibility for the future of these areas. The other half of the land is in private hands. Here the lumber companies, the livestock owners, the farmers, and the real-estate developers are the groups in whose hands the future rests. Over these privately owned lands the various governments, town, city, county, and state, can exercise varying degrees of control. The state, particularly through its natural-resources agency that includes the Department of Water Resources, and through its Highway Commission, can exert the most important influence on all private activities, and therefore bears the greatest responsibility for future trends.

Of the various private groups, I believe that the lumber companies, much maligned though they may be, have been the most conservation-minded, in the broad sense of the world. I feel also that the real-estate developers, although some have been exemplary in their activities, have

been the least responsive to the public interest. More research is obviously needed, if these private groups are to do an adequate job, and much of this must be sponsored by public agencies. We need further knowledge of forest and range management to make possible a more responsible use of these lands. We need much more work on the problems of agricultural pest control, to prevent the poisoning of our environment through pesticides. We need more work on economic means for the disposal of the waste products of industries and cities, to avoid further pollution of water and air. More government control is still needed to prevent permanent damage to the land by those groups that still seek a quick profit at the expense of the public welfare.

Fortunately, the very population pressure that threatens to destroy California has set in motion counterforces of conservation that can save it. Most of all we need a vision, an ideal, of what the state can be—a land that would permit the greatest diversity of human activities and the fullest expression of human freedom in a setting of natural splendor and man-made beauty—a place where technology is made to work for the interests of humanity, and man is not forced into a warped mold to suit the requirements of the computer. California can be a model that all the world would admire. It can set an example that all other regions will try to follow. But unless we act now to stop the forces of destruction that are at work, the state that once was green and golden may become an object lesson that shows only what other areas must avoid.

Shortly after he died while fighting a brush fire along the Wisconsin River, Aldo Leopold (1886–1948) began to be discussed in a very small circle of ecologists as something of a prophet. His thinking, it was said, was decades—perhaps centuries—ahead of his time. Today Leopold is one of the patron saints of environmentalists, widely known as a philosopher-scientist who points the way out of the morass of egocentricity that has burdened man-environment relations in the western world for centuries. In reading SUSAN LOUISE FLADER'S (b. 1941) summary of the main tenets of Leopold's philosophy, look for the differences between his ideas and those of the Progressive conservationists as well as those of the pioneers. To what extent can you accept Leopold's principles? What do you think would be required for most Americans to adopt a land ethic?

Susan Louise Flader

Aldo Leopold and the Evolution of an Ecological Attitude

On the first day of April 1944, Aldo Leopold sat down with sharpened pencil and a pad of yellow blue-lined paper, prepared to acknowledge in writing that he himself had once felt very differently about what he now regarded as the essence of an ecological attitude.

"A deep chesty bawl echoes from rimrock to rimrock as it rolls down the mountain and fades into the far blackness of the night," he began. "It is an outburst of wild defiant sorrow, and of contempt for all the adversities of the world." The deer, the coyote, the cowman, the hunter, in each the call instilled some immediate

and mortal fear or hope. "Only the mountain," he wrote, "has lived long enough to listen objectively to the howl of a wolf." Though known only to the mountain, the deeper meaning of wolves, as also their very presence or absence, could be sensed by all, Leopold felt, and he described the event by which he himself had begun to sense it—the time, back in his southwestern years [1909–1924], when he shot a wolf and saw it die:

We reached the old wolf in time to watch a fierce green fire dying in her eyes. I realized then, and have known ever since, that there was something new to me in those eyes—some-

From Susan Louise Flader, "Aldo Leopold and the Evolution of an Ecological Attitude (unpublished Ph.D. dissertation, Stanford University, 1971), pp. 1–3, 34–35, 36, 37–39, 43–45. Copyright 1971 by Susan Louise Flader.

thing known only to her and to the mountain. I was young then, and full of trigger-itch; I thought that because fewer wolves meant more deer, that no wolves would mean hunters' paradise. But after seeing the green fire die, I sensed that neither the wolf nor the mountain agreed with such a view.

In [this essay, which he entitled] "Thinking Like a Mountain," Aldo Leopold compressed into one dramatic moment a realization that had required years. . . . The wolf, as one of the large carnivores, belonged at the very apex of the biotic pyramid, the image employed in ecology to represent the energy circuit of nature. Through millenia of evolution the pyramid had increased in height and complexity, and this elaboration and diversification, in Leopold's thinking, contributed to the smooth functioning, or health, of the system. Man with his arrogance and his engines of violence now presumed, in his solicitude for deer and cattle, to lop off the large carnivores from the apex of the pyramid, for the first time in history making food chains shorter and less diverse, and thus disorganizing the system. The wolf, standing at the apex of the pyramid, became a symbol of the pyramid itself, of land health. Leopold did not elaborate this symbolism in "Thinking Like a Mountain," but it is there. It is the hidden meaning in the howl of the wolf. One who could listen objectively to that howl—who could visualize the wolf in its relation to the total life process of the ecosystem through time, not just as it might affect one's own immediate interests—was thinking ecologically, like a mountain. . . .

The term ecology is usually credited to the German biologist Ernst Haeckel, who coined it in 1866 of two Greek words: *oikos,* meaning household or living relations, and *logos,* study of. He defined it as "the whole science of the relations of the organism to the environment including, in the broad sense, all the 'conditions of existence;'" and he used the term in his efforts to interpret to the scientific world of Germany the significance of Charles Darwin's theory of natural selection and evolution and his concept of "the economy of nature," as presented in the *Origin of Species* (1859). To Darwin, rather than to Haeckel, belongs the principal credit for describing the complex functional interrelatedness of organisms and environment, and the tendency of the evolutionary process to elaborate and diversify the biota and produce what ecologists today speak of as a system in dynamic equilibrium. In the furor over the very fact of evolution and the religious and social implications of the animal origins of man, however, the ecological implications of evolutionary thought were all but lost. . . .

Ecology as a self-conscious scientific discipline is a child of the twentieth century. In the United States around the turn of the century it was plant ecology that gained attention and set the style for ensuing decades, with the work of Frederic E. Clements on "plant formations" and "climax" vegetation in the state of Nebraska and Henry C. Cowles' studies of vegetational succession on the sand dunes of Lake Michigan. Strongly influenced by the conceptual frameworks and investigative techniques developed by the Cowles and Clements schools of plant ecology, early animal ecologists like V. E. Shelford and C. C. Adams contented themselves largely with filling in the animals in the successional picture. The approach of all these people was primarily descriptive rather than functional. . . .

As a student at Yale [1904–1909], Aldo Leopold would undoubtedly have been exposed to the new ecological concepts emanating from Chicago and Nebraska, particularly as they described the distribution and succession of forest types, but his thinking would probably not have been dominated by them. Every bit as important as origins for his ecological thinking were his habit of keen observation and his historical curiosity, coupled with his voracious reading of the great naturalists, from [Henry David] Thoreau to Joseph Grinnell, and the journals of the early explorers.

Leopold may be said to have been thinking ecologically—holistically . . .— even before ecological science had evolved a conceptual framework capable of supporting such thought. At a time when leading plant ecologists were still describing normal successional stages as a response to average environmental factors, Leopold through careful observation and inferential reasoning arrived at an essentially functional interpretation of vegetation change and soil erosion on southwestern watersheds . . . which integrated soils, vegetation, topography and climate, geologic and human history, lightning fires and livestock grazing into a single system of interactions. He was left with a profound respect for the fragile equilibrium of the arid Southwest, in which man's activities in one part of the system were capable of inducing massive, sometimes progressive, usually unanticipated and too often unrecognized changes in other parts of the system. It was an environment set, as he termed it, on "hair-trigger." As a land manager, he was concerned with the implications of his interpretation for human action. Action involved changes not only in patterns of land use, but also in institutional arrangements affecting land use and, even more fundamentally, in the perceptions, attitudes, and values of a people. Leopold saw all this at least as early as 1923. . . .

Casting about for philosophical underpinnings for his interpretation of the hair-trigger equilibrium in the Southwest, he hit upon the organicism of the Russian philosopher P. D. Ouspensky, who regarded the whole earth and the smallest particle thereof as a living being, possessed of soul or consciousness. "Possibly, in our intuitive perceptions, which may be truer than our science and less impeded by words than our philosophies," Leopold wrote, "we realize the indivisibility of the earth—its soil, mountains, rivers, forests, climate, plants, and animals, and respect it collectively not only as a useful servant but as a living being." Leopold never published this first attempt at formulating a conservation philosophy. In later years, as ecological science became more functional and holistic, he would begin to couch his land ethic in ecological concepts, rather than in the terminology of the philosophers. . . .

The 1930s were productive years in the biological sciences, especially in the realms of ecological and evolutionary theory. Evolution and ecology were coming to be recognized as two windows on the same process.

Ecological science, as it became more functional during the 1930s and early 1940s, provided Leopold with the concept of the biotic community, or land, as "a fountain of energy flowing through a circuit of soils, plants and animals," an energy circuit which could be symbolized as a biotic pyramid. . . . Energy relations were continuous through time as well as in space. The trend of evolution was to elaborate and diversify the biota, to add layer upon layer to the pyramid, link after link to the food chains (energy channels) of which it was composed. There was a definite relationship, it seemed to . . . Leopold, between the complex structure and the smooth functioning of the whole —between the evolution of ecological diversity and the capacity of the land organism for self-renewal, which [he] termed stability or land health.

The objective of conservation, in a system thus understood, was to preserve the capacity for healthy functioning of the system, rather than primarily to protect individual members . . . or to give a competitive advantage to certain "desirable" species over others less desired, as in early game management [Leopold's own profession]. Three decades of experience trying to "control" wildlife populations by manipulating selected environmental factors had had a profoundly sobering effect on Leopold. A proper function of management, it now became apparent to him, was to encourage the greatest possible diversity in an attempt to preserve the widest possible realm in which natural processes might seek their own equilibrium. "A thing is right," he ventured in his essay "The Land Ethic," written late in 1947 as the capstone of *Sand County Almanac,* "when it tends to preserve the integrity, stability and beauty of the biotic community. It is wrong when it tends otherwise."

These values, integrity (or co-evolved diversity), stability, and beauty, were fundamental to Leopold's thinking from the beginning. But, like his notion of a land ethic, they acquired new meanings and implications throughout his life in response to his changing perception of the environment.

Suggestions for Further Reading

Writings about the environment are currently multiplying at a rate that frustrates even the most avid reader. But by restricting concern to environmental *history* the task becomes more manageable.

A good place to begin further exploration of the field is the comprehensive histories. One of the most readable is Stewart L. Udall's *The Quiet Crisis* (New York, 1963), a portion of which appears in this volume. The rest of Udall's account focuses on the rise of conservation as both an idea and a multi-faceted institution. The book is available in an inexpensive paperback edition, while the hardbound edition contains a wealth of illustrative material. *The Conservationists* (Reading, Mass., 1971) by Douglas H. Strong is a convenient short review, in paperback, of the prime movers in this field. David Cushman Coyle's *Conservation: An American Story of Conflict and Accomplishment* (New Brunswick, N.J., 1957) is an engineer's undocumented but usually reliable survey. More polemical in tone are two histories by former United States Congressmen: Robert S. Kerr, *Land, Wood and Water* (New York, 1960) and Frank E. Smith, *The Politics of Conservation* (New York, 1966). Judson King's *The Conservation Fight: From Theodore Roosevelt to the Tennessee Valley Authority* (Washington, D.C., 1959) and Ernest F. Swift, *A Conservation Saga* (Washington, D.C., 1967) are historical reminiscences by men close to the mainstream of the conservation movement.

Several edited collections have simplified the researcher's labors. Henry Clepper (ed.), *Origins of American Conservation* (New York, 1966) brings together short, historical sketches by leaders in various fields of resource management. Another group effort is Henry Jarrett's (ed.), *Perspectives on Conservation:* *Essays on America's Natural Resources* (Baltimore, 1958). Environmental history can also be learned from the primary documents. Convenient collections are Frank Smith (ed.), *Conservation in the United States: A Documentary History* (5 vols., New York, 1971) and Roderick Nash (ed.), *The American Environment: Readings in the History of Conservation* (Reading, Mass., 1968). The latter, which is in paperback, contains an extensive bibliography. It should be supplemented with Gordon B. Dodds, "The Historiography of American Conservation: Past and Present," *Pacific Northwest Quarterly, LVI* (1965), 75–81. Two new collections are John Opre, ed., *Americans and Environment: The Controversy Over Ecology* (Lexington, Mass., 1971) and Frank Graham, Jr., *Man's Dominion: The Story of Conservation in America* (New York 1971).

A number of scholarly works attempt to trace the outlines of American attitude toward the environment. Hans Huth, *Nature and the American: Three Centuries of Changing Attitude* (Berkeley, Cal., 1957) is strongest in analyzing the growth of appreciation of natural beauty in the eighteenth and nineteenth centuries. The book contains a large number of illustrations. Broader and more insightful is Arthur A. Ekirch, Jr., *Man and Nature in America* (New York, 1963). A sample of Ekirch's approach may be obtained in the present volume. *Wilderness and the American Mind* (New Haven, Conn., 1967) by Roderick Nash is concerned with American attitudes and conduct toward a particular environment. The book is available in a paperbound edition as is Henry Nash Smith's *Virgin Land: The American West as Symbol and Myth*. A pioneer interpreter of the symbolic significance of American literature, Smith recognizes the difference between perception and reality with respect to environment. Leo Marx, *The Machine in the Garden: Technology and the Pastoral Ideal in America* (New York, 1964) also uses imaginative writing as document in discussing the central environmental issue in 19th-century American thought. Peter J. Schmitt's *Back to Nature: The Arcadian Myth in Urban America* (New York, 1969) focuses on popular thought. The serious student will also want to see Howard Mumford Jones, *O Strange New World* (New York, 1964), Charles L. Sanford, *The Quest for Paradise* (Urbana, Ill., 1961) and Arthur K. Moore, *The Frontier Mind: A Cultural Analysis of the Kentucky Frontiersman* (Lexington, Ky., 1957). For American thought regarding the urban environment Morton and Lucia White, *The Intellectual Versus the City* (Cambridge, Mass., 1962) is a good place to start.

Environmental history often lies buried in seemingly unrelated bodies of material. For instance, Ray Harvey Pearce, *The Savages of America: A Study of the Indian and the Idea of Civilization* (Baltimore, 1965) is a rich source of information about American hopes and fears with respect to wildness in both man and nature. John Thomas Flexner, *That Wilder Image: The Painting of America's Native School from Thomas Cole to Winslow Homer* (Boston, 1962) discusses environmental attitudes as they are reflected in painting. For poetry and fiction we have Wilson O. Clough, *The Necessary Earth: Nature and Solitude in American Literature* (Austin, Texas, 1964) and Edwin Russell, *Frontier: American Literature and the American West* (Princeton, N. J., 1965).

Some of the most important secondary writings about environment and Americans are of essay length. One thinks of Russel B. Nye's "The American View of Nature" in his *This Almost Chosen People: Essays in the History of American Ideas* (East Lansing, Mich., 1966) and of Perry Miller's, "Nature and the National Ego" in his *Errand into the Wilderness* (Cambridge, Mass., 1956). Miller includes several other seminal essays in his *Nature's Nation* (Cambridge, Mass., 1967). Another perceptive thrust into the subject is David

Lowenthal's "The American Image of Nature as Virtue," *Landscape,* IX (1959–60), 16–26. Douglas Strong has created a readable synthesis in "The Rise of American Esthetic Conservation: Muir, Mather, and Udall," *National Parks Magazine,* XLIV (1970), 5–9.

Professional historians of American conservation are not numerous, but several pathbreaking interpretations of limited periods are available. Samuel P. Hays, *Conservation and the Gospel of Efficiency: The Progressive Conservation Movement, 1890–1920* (Cambridge, Mass., 1959) is the standard account of this seminal period. J. Leonard Bates, "Fulfilling American Democracy: The Conservation Movement, 1907–1921," *Mississippi Valley Historical Review,* 44 (1957), 29–57 and Roderick Nash, "The American Cult of the Primitive," *American Quarterly,* 18 (Fall, 1966), 517–537 offer alternative interpretations to that of Hays. In *The Politics of Conservation: Crusades and Controversies, 1897–1913* (Berkeley, 1962), Elmo R. Richardson has examined the often-violent interaction of varying conservation philosophies in the Progressive years.

Taking up where the Hays book ends, Donald C. Swain's *Federal Conservation Policy, 1921–1933* (Berkeley, 1963) is a thorough study of national developments. Swain's *Horace M. Albright and Conservation* (Chicago, 1970) carries part of the conservation story into recent years. Other treatments of recent environmental history may be found in Paul Brooks, *The Pursuit of Wilderness* (Boston, 1971), Richard A. Cooky and Geoffrey Wandesforde-Smith, eds., *Congress and the Environment* (Seattle, 1970), and in Elmo Richardson's "Dams, Parks, and Politics: Resource Development and Preservation in the Truman-Eisenhower Era" soon to be published in book form.

Histories of the public domain and federal land policy inevitably concern the American environment and attitude toward it. The best works are Roy M. Robbins, *Our Landed Heritage: The Public Domain, 1776–1936* (Princeton, 1942), E. Louise Peffer, *The Closing of the Public Domain: Disposal and Reservation Policies, 1900–1950* (Stanford, 1951), and Vernon Carstensen, ed., *The Public Lands: Studies in the History of the Public Domain* (Madison, Wis., 1963).

Among the many works of limited scope the following might be singled out as particularly valuable for the student of American priorities regarding the environment: Arthur Maass, *Muddy Waters: The Army Engineers and the Nation's Rivers* (Cambridge, Mass., 1951); Michael Frome, *Whose Woods These Are: The Story of the National Forests* (Garden City, N.Y., 1962); John Ise, *Our National Park Policy: A Critical History* (Baltimore, 1961); James L. Penick, *Progressive Politics and Conservation: The Ballinger-Pinchot Affair* (Chicago, 1968); John A. Salmond, *The Civilian Conservation Corps, 1933–1942: A New Deal Case Study* (Durham, N.C., 1967); Gordon R. Clapp, *The TVA: An Approach to the Development of a Region* (Chicago, 1955); James B. Trefethen, *Crusade for Wildlife* (Harrisburg, Pa., 1961), and Arthur E. Morgan, *Dams and Other Disasters* (Boston, 1971).

Some writers have focused on the interaction of man and land in particular regions. Often their findings can be extrapolated to shed light on the broader subject of Americans and environment. Readers who found the selection from Raymond Dasmann in the present collection useful will want to read his account of California's environmental history in its entirety. William O. Douglas has written a similar study in *Farewell to Texas: A Vanishing Wilderness* (New York, 1967), while Richard G. Lillard's *Eden in Jeopardy* (New York, 1966) concerns a region within a region —southern California. A model of regional environmental history is Michael Frome's *Strangers in High Places: The Story of the Great Smoky Mountains* (New York, 1966).

William C. White also focuses on a mountain environment in *Adirondack Country* (New York, 1954) as does Francis P. Farquhar in *History of the Sierra Nevada* (Berkeley, 1965). Walter P. Webb's *The Great Plains* (Boston, 1931) and James C. Malin's *The Grassland of North America* (Lawrence, Kansas, 1961) treat the land between the Mississippi River and the Rocky Mountains.

Biographies of Americans who figured prominently in the conservation movement offer another approach to environmental history. David Lowenthal's *George Perkins Marsh: Versatile Vermonter* (New York, 1958) and Wallace Stegner's *Beyond the Hundredth Meridian: John Wesley Powell and the Second Opening of the West* (Boston, 1954) are masterpieces. The lives and thoughts of two men who clashed bitterly over environmental priorities are documented in Linnie Marsh Wolfe, *Son of the Wilderness: The Life of John Muir* (New York, 1945) and M. *Gifford Pinchot: Private and Public Forester Politician* (Princeton, 1960). Harold T. Pinkett has recently published another biography, *Gifford Pinchot: Private and Public Forester* (Urbana, Ill., 1970). A tripartite biography with sensitive treatment of the meaning of environment is Edward White's *The Eastern Establishment and the Western Experience: The West of Frederic Remington, Theodore Roosevelt, and Owen Wister* (New Haven, 1968).

An important repository of environmental history are the files of periodicals in the field. Among the most helpful are *Forest History, Living Wilderness, Sierra Club Bulletin* (the early years of the journal are indexed), *American Forests, Audubon, Natural History, National Wildlife,* and *National Parks and Conservation Magazine.*